Margot Terry

To Margo

May wisdo[illegible]
your path to our Fathers
house.
with love from the heart
E. J.

THE OPENING OF THE WISDOM-EYE

THIS important book by His Holiness the XIVth Dalai Lama gives an authentic account of the teachings of Tibetan Buddhism. It is hoped that its publication will contribute to a greater understanding of Tibetan culture.

The main part of the book is preceded by a short account of the spread of Buddhism in Tibet, also written by His Holiness. The whole range of Buddhist teachings as practiced in Tibet is expounded with great clarity, yet with brevity.

The work has been translated from the Tibetan language by three Buddhist scholars who worked together at a Buddhist temple in Thailand: Thubten Kalzang Rinpoche from Tibet, a noted scholar of Sanskrit and Hindi; Bhikkhu Nagasena of India, whose knowledge of Pali and Siamese has earned him the title of *Phra Maha*; and Bhikkhu Khantipalo of England, whose books include *Buddhism Explained* and *Tolerance.*

The work is attractively illustrated with photographs.

Avalokitesvara, in Tibetan, Chenrezi, in the form Simhanada, the Lion's Roar symbolic of fearlessness in proclaiming the Truth. Chenrezi is the Bodhisattva symbolizing compassion and incarnates in the succession of Dalai Lamas of Tibet.

THE OPENING OF THE WISDOM-EYE

AND THE

HISTORY OF THE ADVANCEMENT OF BUDDHADHARMA IN TIBET

BY

HIS HOLINESS TENZIN GYATSHO
THE XIVth DALAI LAMA OF TIBET

A QUEST BOOK

Published under a grant from The Kern Foundation

THE THEOSOPHICAL PUBLISHING HOUSE
Wheaton, Ill., U.S.A.
Madras, India / London, England

U.S.A. edition 1972

This edition published by The Theosophical Publishing House, Wheaton, Illinois, a department of The Theosophical Society in America, by arrangement with His Holiness Tenzin Gyatsho, the XIVth Dalai Lama of Tibet

Library of Congress Catalog Card Number 70-152732

ISBN: 0-8356-0202-8

Printed in the United States of America

CONTENTS

THE INTRODUCTION OF HIS HOLINESS THE DALAI LAMA

I HAVE written this small book keeping in mind the needs of people, both those living in the East and those in the West, who wish to find the right way and gain knowledge of the teaching (Dharma) of Lord Buddha. His Dharma is indeed deep like an ocean and while expounding it he has used many skillful-means, an expression of his All-knowledge. In later times, the great and wise teachers in India developed some additional skillful-means and in this book I have tried to present both the original as well as the later developments, laying aside the philosophical subtleties and points of controversy while concentrating upon matters of practical application.

The efforts of the Council for Cultural and Religious Affairs in publishing this book are indeed greatly appreciated.

GELONG TENZIN GYATSHO,
the XIVth Dalai Lama.

Full Moon Day of the 3rd Tibetan month in the 937th year of the Rabjyong Era*
(8th May, 1963)

* From the introduction of Kālacakra (the Wheel of Time) into Tibet. In His Holiness' name 'Gelong' is the Tibetan equivalent of Bhikṣu, or fully ordained Buddhist monk.

THE TRANSLATORS' PREFACE

THIS book of His Holiness the Dalai Lama has been written with the intention of giving information to those wishing to know some of the basic facets of Buddhadharma in Tibet. Further, it touches upon a number of points of practical importance for those who wish to progress along the path of Dharma, while it should incidentally set right a number of distorted and strange ideas that some people have regarding Tibetan forms of Dharma.

The translators would like, in this preface, to make a few random points for the convenience of readers. Firstly, there is the way in which the book came to be translated and the actual method of translation. Last year, (2508/1965) during the Rains Residence, three bhikkhus met regularly at Wat Bovoranives (monastery) for the translation of some small Buddhist works from Tibetan. In this team, Ven. Thubten Kalsang Rinpoche is from Tibet, Ven. Nagasena from India and the writer* from England. Some of the fruits of their labors appeared in a book called *The Wisdom Gone Beyond* (published by the Social Science Press of Thailand, Bangkok), among the contents of which are the translations from Tibetan of *The Letter of Kindheartedness* (*Suhṛllekha*) of Ācārya Nāgārjuna, and two books of Dharma-similes entitled *Trees and Water*. Having completed these, the translators wondered what other works might be attempted.

* Bhikkhu Khantipalo.

The book translated here had been written in Tibetan some time before by His Holiness the Dalai Lama and was soon translated into Hindi after many had requested that this Dharma be made available to the Indian peoples. Kazi Sonam Topgay, interpreter to His Holiness, had set to work to render the whole book into English though this was not completed. It was at this juncture that Ven. Thubten Kalsang Rinpoche, who was in contact with His Holiness and who received from the Council for Cultural and Religious Affairs of H. H. the Dalai Lama both the Hindi translation and the partial English one, approached Ven. Nagasena and the writer with the request that we help to translate this work into English. Thus it came about that for our purpose of translation, Ven. Rinpoche held the Tibetan text, my venerable friend Bhikkhu Nagasena had charge of the Hindi, while the writer had the English typescript. Of the two latter versions, the Hindi translation of a venerable Lama in India with the editing of a famous Sanskrit pandit, showed considerable tendency to elaborate, sometimes at great length, statements which, in the original were quite brief. However, this was often an advantage as the Tibetan original seems to have been very tersely written in many places so that we have incorporated a number of these explanatory portions where we felt that they would be required by readers of the English version. We also found in the Hindi translation some turns of phrase which looked rather Hindi and as these, when checked with Tibetan, could not be found, so care has been taken to omit them here.

On the other hand, the English translation in typescript and about three-quarters complete, stays close to the brevity of the original but as the translaton needed extensive amplification and correct equivalents for Buddhist terms, some care was needed in its use. However, occasional sentences and phrases have been taken straight from the work where they expressed the meaning well.

As to the actual method of translating, it proceeded like this: Venerable Rinpoche and Ven. Bhikkhu Nagasena would come to the writer's room in this wat at a pre-arranged time. The former would have prepared his own Hindi rendering, being more conversant with that language than with English, from the original Tibetan which, sentence by sentence, was checked with the printed Hindi translation by Ven. Nagasena. This gave rise from time to time, to discussions on points obscure or difficult, a few of which could not be solved in Siam but were only unraveled finally in India when the typescript was returned to His Holiness the Dalai Lama for checking. The translation work continued with Ven. Nagasena reading out a literal rendering in English which retained all the Buddhist technical terms in Sanskrit, most of which were familiar to us. This literal translation together with any explanatory matter thought to be necessary was then written down in the present writer's brief notation. In these penciled hieroglyphs it remained until after the opening of the temple established by the Thai Government and Saṅgha in London. Upon the writer's return, he wrote it up in, what it is hoped will be found, readable English. The whole work was then written out again incorporating corrections both in content and style, as well as adding to the notes. My venerable friend, Bhikkhu Pasadiko, has painstakingly gone through the book suggesting further improvements and correcting inaccuracies in the Sanskrit diacritics. The final translation has been checked by Ven. Rato Rinpoche and Mr. Gyatsho Tshering of the Council for Cultural and Religious Affairs of H. H. the Dalai Lama.

Something should now be said of the notes. They are, with the exception of the second one and a few others, all the responsibility of the present writer—and he craves the pardon of scholars for shortcomings in this respect. Those few which have not been made by him are the work of the Venerable translator of the Hindi edition. In these notes, besides explaining points obviously requiring further expansion, an attempt has been made to relate, usually by comparison but occasionally by contrast, the ways and categories of the Dharma in Tibet with those found in Theravāda. The reason for this is not only the feeling among many Buddhists that we have much more in common than divides us—that in fact we can distinguish a great mass of basic and practical teachings which we may well call "Root-Dharma," but also that many people are comparatively familiar with the translations from the Pāli Canon (Tripiṭaka). This is particularly true of the vast store of Discourses of Lord Buddha preserved there and which form the basis for both Theravāda teachings and those of Sarvāstivāda tradition as still taught from such works as the famous *Abhidharmakośa*. References have therefore been given to these Discourses (Sutta) where identical or similar topics are dealt with in this work.

As to the pictures which adorn the book, it has been our aim to select illustrations of Tibetan Buddhism being practiced in as many ways as possible. One may find illustrations in western books of Tibetan art and culture but usually not of Dharma-practice. We have tried to rectify this omission. The colored plates of thankas, photographed in Siam, having very kindly been brought out of India when His Holiness and retinue visited this country, show various styles described in the text on the plates.

Then there is the question of how to deal with the technical terms in this work translated from Tibetan into Sanskrit. These have usually been left in the body of the text with, it is hoped, an adequate English translation. Familiarity with at least the basic terms commonly used in the Dharma is essential and as many of these cannot be very accurately rendered into English, so their Sanskrit originals should be remembered and an effort made to understand their range of meaning. It has happened in a few cases that they have been left untranslated (Buddha, Dharma, dharma, duhkha, etc.) with notes upon their first occurrence. Repeated use, in any case, soon makes one familiar with these few terms. English is not adequate for some of the terms common to the Buddhist training but we may expect, should the Dharma increase in English-speaking lands, that the English language will absorb more and more of these terms, as the languages of the Buddhist East have already done.

Now a word as to the reading and arrangement of this book. " The History of the Advance of the Dharma in Tibet " which forms an appendix in the Hindi edition is here inserted before the main work itself, with the idea that it will form an easy beginning to this book. Readers who do not have much knowledge of Buddhist teachings will find no difficulty in this section. Having read it, the writer suggests that they turn first to the sections on " Dharma " and then to the " Threefold Training " which comprises Virtues, Collectedness and Wisdom. When this material has been read carefully—and the Wisdom section particularly requires this—the reader may turn back to the beginning of the book and then read it through in due order. This book will repay reading several times, and should one know any teacher competent to explain it, many of the subjects compressed into short sections here, may be illumined by him in all the marvelous profundity of the Dharma.

Anyone who has studied the Dharma will realize that it is a technical subject because the matter with which it deals—mind and body and their training in the path to enlightenment—is complex and requires an exact and technical approach. Complications are sometimes unavoidable since the generality of men are themselves complications of greed, aversion and delusion. The ways of training oneself and thereby of benefiting others which will be described here, are actually basic to all forms of the Dharma. They are good examples of the Root Dharma which is the common heritage of both Theravāda and Mahāyāna, for it is on the grounds of practice where harmony between seemingly divergent traditions may be sought. Practices when closely examined are after all, not so widely different as the books alone would suggest.

Practice in fact, not just belief, forms the essence of Buddhist Dharma. Here and now, in daily life or in retreat, as bhikkhu or nun, as upāsaka or upāsikā (layman and laywoman), one may practice Dharma if he wishes. And what briefly is this practice? The first steps are:

> " *Restraint from evil and*
> *Increase of the skillful.*"

One achieves the first by taking the precepts and then maintaining them with sincerity and impurity. The second aspect is accomplished through very ordinary but very essential things, such as generosity toward those whom one should support, helpfulness for those in need of assistance, respect for those who should be respected, and gentleness toward all living creatures, human or non-human. One can never neglect these steps in favor of intellectual study. No amount of book-work, or of lectures, will replace the need for increasing the skillful in one's own heart. Merit (puṇya), or " that which cleanses and purifies " is the basis of all Buddhist practice everywhere and every opportunity ought to be used to the greatest advantage for the increase of the skillful and decrease of evil, for this is the Path of Purity and without it no enlightenment can be expected. Books and lectures are a means of getting information. Having gained the necessary facts, one should try to find a good teacher who can explain how to apply the gathered facts to one's life. Practice never can be fulfilled through knowledge of books alone but only by application of Dharma to one's daily life. Necessarily therefore, a Buddhist is one who develops in himself generosity, helpfulness, reverence, gentleness, patience, contentment and so forth, and in whom these qualities can be seen, but while he may be learned as well, this will not be true of all good Buddhists.

Secondly, Buddhist practice means the training and development of the mind-and-heart (citta) which is often called " meditation " but is here more accurately known as " collectedness." However, this cannot be undertaken successfully unless purity of mind has first been established to some extent by " Restraint from evil and increase of the skillful."

As with all other sorts of training, in the Dharma first things come first, and if one is in doubt where to begin, one cannot do better than to practice restraint and merit-making which is indeed to begin at the beginning.

It is the earnest wish of the translators that the Dharma of the Greatly Compassionate One may penetrate to the hearts of all wise men. And soon, very soon, we trust, may the Tibetan peoples gain freedom from oppression so that they may once again practice the Dharma.

HISTORY OF THE ADVANCEMENT OF BUDDHADHARMA IN TIBET

IN Tibet, the supreme teaching of Lord Buddha is followed everywhere. As there are numbers of misunderstandings found regarding the practice by Tibetans of the Dharma, we feel it necessary to present here a brief history of the advancement of the Dharma in our country.

Geographically, Tibet is divided into three main regions which comprise U-Tsang, Do-Töd and Do-Mēd. Not one place can be found in these three regions to which the Buddhadharma has not spread, so that we say this Dharma shines giving light like the sun over all the land of Tibet.

From the point of view of time, the history of Tibet falls into two parts: the ancient advancement of the Sāsana (teaching), and then the later advancement.

THE ANCIENT ADVANCEMENT

The thirty-second king of Tibet was Srong-tsen-Ganpo (d. 650 C.E.), ascending the throne at the age of thirteen and ruling very religiously thereafter. It was due to him that the Dharma first reached Tibet, and through his efforts number of temples were constructed in Lhasa, Tra-Drug (South Tibet) and at other places. Then he sent his counselor, Thon-mi-Sambhota to study in India where he became proficient in grammar and in the various Indian scripts. Returning to Tibet, he composed upon the model of what he had learnt, a script and eight volumes of grammar and orthography suitable for Tibetan.

This king invited many wise and learned Indian and Nepalese Buddhist pandits to visit Tibet. Among those who went there in his reign, the most famous were Ācārya (teacher) Kumāra, Ācārya Brahmanaśaṅkara, and Ācārya Śīlamañju, of Nepal. These teachers translated the original teaching in the Discourses (Sūtra), or rather some of them, together with some Tantra (texts for meditation practice) and so introduced Buddhist teaching to the Tibetans. Although the Dharma was not taught widely, the king himself guided many fortunate people especially in the teaching of the Mahākaruṇika (The Greatly Compassionate One, or Avalokiteśvara).

After this wise king, the thirty-seventh ruler was styled king Tri-tsong-de-tsen (756-804 C.E.), another very righteous and pious ruler. In his mind was the very strong intention to spread Buddhadharma throughout his realm for which purpose he also invited Indian Buddhist teachers. It was because of his invitation that the leading teachers, Upadhyāya Śāntarakṣita and Guru Padma-sambhāva, went to Tibet. Among others who went, we may mention here ācārya(s): Vimalamitra, Śāntigarbha, Dharmakīrti, Buddhaguhya, Kamalaśīla, Vibuddhasiddha. These great learned teachers and many more are well known in Tibet by the name of the 108 pandits. They translated many works into Tibetan working in conjunction with teachers in Tibet such as Vairocana, Nyag Jyānakumāra, Kawa Pal-Tseg and Chogro Lu Gyaltsen. The three main divisions of the Sacred Canon of the Buddha-word (the Tripiṭaka), called the Discipline, Discourses and Psychophilosophy (Vinaya, Sūtra and Abhidharma) together with Tāntric teachings and many of the main commentaries, became in this way, available in the Tibetan language. At the same time, these learned teachers also established vihāras (monastic residences) as seats of learning and places for practice.

The next great ruler after king Tri-tsong-de-tsen, was the forty-first in Tibetan history, styled king Tri-ral-pa-tsen (817-836 C.E.). In his reign he appointed for each bhikṣu * (monk), seven families for his support, also building over one thousand vihāras. He was so greatly filled with trust in the Buddhadharma, that he made his teachers (ācārya and guru) stand on the ends of his headcloth whereupon he worshipped them whole-heartedly. He indeed served the teaching of the conquerors in a noble way. As in the case of the two previous kings, he also invited Indian Buddhist teachers to Tibet and among those who went in his reign were

* [Also bhikkhu.]

the ācārya and upadhyāya(s): Jinamitra, Surendrabodhi, Sīlendrabodhi, Dānaśīla, and so on. The king also allowed the Tibetan upadhyāya(s) Ratnarakṣita and Dharmatāśīla with the lotsava(s) or translators Jñānasena and Jayarakṣita to revise the old translations done in the days of previous kings (which had since proved to be obscure) and to settle on the most correct Tibetan words for the Sanskrit terms so far untranslated both in the books of the disciples (śrāvaka) and in those of the Mahāyāna (Great Vehicle). These pandits then prepared, with the permission of the king, an edition in sixteen volumes of the work known as the "Great Mother," that is in Sanskrit: Śatasahasrika-prajñāpāramitā-sūtra (the discourse in one hundred-thousand [verses] upon Perfect Wisdom). Likewise, the old translations of the Buddha-word were revised and re-written in the language of those times thus giving impetus to the Wheel of Dharma in the 'Land of Snows.' This ends the brief account of the ancient period of Dharma-advancement.

THE LATER ADVANCEMENT

After the death of the last monarch, the forty-second styled king Lang-dar-ma (836-842 C.E.) hated Buddhist teachings. He committed many outrages against Buddhist vihāras and treated Buddhists with great cruelty so that the Buddhaśāsana very nearly disappeared during his reign. Fearing this king, three followers from the tradition of Ācārya Śāntarakṣita fled to the Khamba region in Eastern Tibet and there gained the acceptance as bhikṣus (Buddhist monks) with a preceptor. From this time on, the number of bhikṣus gradually increased again, besides which the acarya(s) Dharmapāla and Sādhupāla from Eastern India moved from western to central Tibet. As a result of these teachers' activities, together with the arrival of Mahāpaṇḍita Śākyaśrī from Kashmir, bhikṣus again increased in numbers so that Buddhadharma was re-established in Tibet.

From that time onwards, Indian teachers went to Tibet, while many translator-teachers of Tibet with great sufferings and many difficulties went down to India and Nepal to study the Sūtra and the Tantra, offering heaps of gold at the feet of the great teachers and sages of that time. Upon their return to Tibet, they translated those teachings into Tibetan so that followers increased there. In this way they opposed the long decline in the traditions of both study and of practice. Due to this, the Buddhasāsana again began to shine like the sun. This is a brief account of the later period of Dharma-advancement in Tibet.

THE VARIOUS BUDDHIST SCHOOLS

There are many Buddhist schools in Tibet and they are named in various ways, that is according to time, place, teaching or founder. For instance, the Nyingma-pa (the Ancient Ones) are named from the point of view of time. Sakya-pa, Stag-lung-pa, Dri-Kung-pa,

Drug-pa, Gedan-pa, are examples of schools named after places. Karma-kargyut-pa and Vuluk-pa commemorate their founders, while Khadam-pa, Zogchen-pa, Tsyag-chen-pa and Shi-je-pa are so named after their respective teachings. All these schools may, however, be divided into two groups: Nying-ma (the Ancient) and Sarma (the New).

What difference is to be found between these two? When Mahāyāna spread to Tibet, it was of two kinds consisting of the Sūtra and of the Tantra but here " old " and " new " refer only to the latter. From ancient times down to the arrival of the acārya Smṛtijñāna, the Tantra-books translated are called the " old translations " and those who follow this teaching are known as the Ancient or Old-style Ones. But from the time of lotsava Rinchen-zangpo onwards, the Tantras rendered into Tibetan were called the " new translations " and its followers, the New-style Ones. This lotsava made the first translation of the new Tantras in 978 C.E. and was followed in the same work by many others. As a result of their efforts the new Tantras and their practice were spread and established in Tibet.

Among the schools found in Tibet up to the present time, four are outstanding. The first of these is in the category of the ancient teachings and is known as Nyingma-pa. The other three are from the new teachings and are known as Kargyut-pa, Sakya-pa and Gelug-pa. We shall introduce each of them briefly.

I. In the year 810 C.E., Ācārya Padma-sambhava of Udyāna went to Tibet. He stayed at the Samye vihāra and there translated eighteen books of the Mahāsiddhi (Great Accomplishment) Tāntric literature dealing with meditation-practice. In the presence of the king and twenty-five other important persons, he set in motion the Adamantine Wheel of the Great Secret (Mahā-rahasya-vajrayāna-cakra). This lineage started by Padmasambhava is known as the Tāntric school of the Ancient Ones (Nyingma-pa).

II. Marpa-lotsava (the translator) was born in 1012 C.E., and during his life visited India three times. In the course of these pilgrimages, under the guidance of the siddhas Naropa and Maitrīpa, he translated and explained authoritative Tāntric books. The tradition founded by him, and by his eminent disciple the Jetsun Milarepa, is called the Kargyut-pa or the Whispered Transmission. This school is divided among eight subschools, four of which are counted as great while four are lesser ones. The former are called: Kam-tsang-pa, Drigung-pa, Taglung-pa and Drug-pa.

III. The year 1034 C.E. saw the birth in Tibet of Kon-chog-gyal-po who in due course listened to the teachings of the lotsava Drogmi explaining the Path and Fruits according to the tradition of the ācārya Dharmapāla. Having practiced he became a great accomplished teacher, known as the Mahāsiddha Vairupa or Mahāpaṇḍita

Gayadhāra. The school initiated by him and developed by his disciples is called the Sakya-pa.

Then in 1039 C.E., Ācārya Mahāpaṇḍita Dīpaṅkara-śrījñāna * from the great vihāra (monastery) of Vikramaśila in India, went to Tibet. There this celebrated teacher expounded at length the deep teachings of both the Sūtra and the Tantra. He established, and his disciples developed, the school called Khadam-pa.

IV. Some three hundred years later, in 1357 C.E., the great being Je Tsong-kha-pa was born and then educated in the Khadam-pa school becoming in time both learned and accomplished in the teachings. He attained to the right meaning of Lord Buddha's words together with their commentaries as transmitted in Tibet, by the wisdoms of hearing, thinking and development. Having gained true knowledge of Lord Buddha's teachings, he taught them to his disciples in a very convincing manner. The school of which he is the founder and which has been developed by the great scholars who followed after him, (such as Khedrub-rje), is known as the Gelug-pa (Virtuous Ones), or the Gedan-pa.

SIMILARITY OF AIMS AMONG THE SCHOOLS

Some people may suppose that since there are many schools of Buddhist thought and practice in Tibet,

* A tradition connects him with Jaiya in the South of Siam where he stayed on his journey to Java.

there must be beliefs, practices and realizations in opposition, just as one finds very clear differences between Buddhists and outsiders. But in truth this is not so.

The differences between Buddhists are only superficial in the same way as there are differences between the aeroplanes we see everyday. Though some are small and some large and though many different designs are seen, still they all fly due to their engines, the presence of air and so forth, all being called "aeroplanes." In the same way, the superficial and minor differences found among the Buddhist schools in Tibet are seen only with regard to the skillful means employed and the methods of practice. Such means and practices have been based on the experiences of the founders and accomplished ones of these various schools, so as to guide trainable men to the right path. The aim of all these schools is the attainment of Buddhahood and in this matter there is no school which differs. Moreover, "skillful-means" here implies the threefold training (in virtue, collectedness and wisdom) and the four seals (mudrā)* to be used for furtherance upon the Path to Buddhahood. These teachings can be used without any contradiction whether one practices the way of the Sūtra, or that of the Tantra, or both together. We should understand that in this way the practices of all the schools are the same.

* All conditioned things are impermanent; all conditioned things are duhkha (unsatisfactory); all dharmas (experiencable events) are without soul or self; and Nirvāṇa is peace.

PRISTINE AND AUTHORITATIVE BUDDHADHARMA IN TIBET

Some persons have the idea that the religion of Tibet is that of the " lamas " who have fabricated a system called " lamaism." They say too, that this is very far from the true teachings of Lord Buddha. Such ideas are very misinformed since there is no separate ' ism ' of the lamas apart from Lord Buddha's teachings.

All the canonical Sūtras and Tantras which form the basis of Buddha-dharma in Tibet were taught by Lord Buddha in person. Again, the Indian scholars made a threefold examination to decide the meaning and authenticity of the Sūtras and Tantras. It should also be known that the great accomplished ones and yogis gained enlightenment by the practice of these deep teachings. Finally, the kings of Tibet who were like bodhisattvas, their eminent ministers and the compassionate translators, had no care even for their own lives, not to speak of money and wealth, in order to gain right knowledge of Dharma. Tibetan scholars suffering many and various hardships on the way to Nepal and India, traveled there many times to get the correct manuscripts and traditions, and their comings and goings could be compared to a river always flowing between two countries. They studied and practiced Dharma under the guidance of the great and learned teachers whose scholarship was beyond question. They satisfied these teachers and the accomplished ones by serving them in every way, listened to their Dharma-teaching and translated this into the Tibetan language. On the basis of those teachings, Tibetan Buddhists listen to Dharma, think upon it and practice it. *Apart from this authentic Dharma there is no arbitrary teaching began by lamas in Tibet.*

If a doubtful point arose among Tibetan pandits, or when some reference had to be searched out in a Dharma-discussion, they would always think, "Was this said by Lord Buddha, or not?" Or perhaps, "Was this teaching given by the Indian pandits, or not?" The Dharma has always been scrutinized in this way. Only on the authority that a statement was made by Lord Buddha, or by the Indian Buddhist teachers, was any teaching considered established and thereby accepted as true.

THE OPENING OF THE WISDOM-EYE

HOMAGE TO SUPREME WISDOM PERFECTLY ANALYZING ALL DHARMAS [1]

ACCORDING to Buddhist tradition, the present era is called the time for virtue (śīla-kāla)[2] being one of the divisions of the five-thousand year period during which, it is said the teaching of the fourth Buddha [3] to appear in this aeon, will actually endure. The most important religious feature of this era therefore lies in the observance of the moral precepts. These are made especially necessary because in this atomic age material progress has been and continues to be very rapid. It is not that this is undesirable but rather that a balance should be struck between material benefits on the one hand, and spiritual values and religious practice on the other. In order to help correct the one-sided emphasis on material matters, the teachings of Lord Buddha can be of great help. These teachings, known to the West as Buddhism but for which we shall use the traditional term "Dharma" have for many centuries been a great mental and spiritual science whereby has been established a well-trodden way for the culture of the mind and heart (both mental and emotional aspects being included in the Buddhist term, " citta ") leading to development in those who wish to practice meditation. It is now that this spiritual heritage should be used for the good of man. The achievement of this would entail many people becoming well versed in Buddhist scriptures and the deep philosophy contained within them. But this would involve a deep and extensive study of these scriptures, which for many people would be difficult in the present, since the sacred books are voluminous while time is often limited. Therefore, it occurred to me that a small book should be produced in which the essence of the Dharma is put down concisely, yet comprehensively. For this reason we have named this work (literally) " The clear Wisdom Eye-opener " and the contents of the chapters following set out this essence of Buddhadharma.

DHARMA[4]

OUR highest duty as human beings is to search out a means whereby beings may be freed from all kinds of sufferings or unsatisfactory experience (duhkha).[5] All living beings desire comfort and happiness and shun sufferings. Moreover, this desire for happiness is not only found in the man of learning and intelligence but among all creatures in the world, even the most insignificant. Whether yourselves, myself, or beings in the animal-world, all wish alike for the increase of pleasure and the diminution of pain. The destruction of this duhkha can only be brought about by making an effort oneself. It is no use to have sublime aspirations but then to sit down and wait for their accomplishment, because this attitude, which is really laziness, will lead neither to the destruction of duhkha nor to the increase of happiness. *It is necessary to stress that all the various aspects of duhkha do in fact arise from causes, thus making it possible to investigate this duhkha and to put an end to it.*

By finding the root-causes of duhkha and then destroying them, human life can become happy and prosperous.

In order to achieve this, it is essential that we practice in our lives those causes producing happiness, while ceasing to operate those causes giving rise to duhkha.

The Dharma of Lord Buddha shows the way to do this. Apart from the Dharma there is no other means whereby we can achieve this objective of happiness and the elimination of sufferings, for in the Dharma, the right method is explained and this brings one who practices to the prefection of his aim. By living according to the Dharma one can make not only this life meaningful, but also those to come, happy and prosperous. To achieve this, one must understand the quintessence of Dharma. When understood this makes a great difference to life such as can be seen between one who lives without Dharma and one who is well established in it. While, for instance, the former will be distressed upon the onset of sickness, thus suffering mentally as well as physically, the latter will react recollecting that such sorts of unsatisfactory experience are natural to life and cannot be avoided. Further, he may consider that duhkha which visits us commonly in the course of life, is in fact the result experienced from past evil karma (past intentional evil actions). Again, he could reflect that his painful feelings are simply the nature of the wandering-on (saṃsāra) in birth and death where such things are bound to be experienced. Thus proportionate to one's knowledge and practice of Dharma, is one's forbearance of duhkha. In other words, it is possible to subdue all physical pains with unhampered ease by sheer strength of mental processes.

All feelings experienced whether pleasurable, painful or neutral, arise from causes and do not arise without causes. As it is said in the treatises (śāstras), pleasure and pain arise due to the workings of the cause and effect principle. A person who is ignorant of Dharma, does not understand this cause and effect and so for him pleasure and pain seem to occur by chance. *The quintessence of Dharma is that one has understood in oneself the causes of one's own duhkha thereby becoming able to tell others of these duhkha-causes.* The true religious man accepts the truth that he is responsible for the pleasurable and unsatisfactory feelings experienced by himself, these being the fruits of his own karma. He knows the fruits of evil, unskillful and harmful karma, are painful, while skillful, beneficial karma results in the experience of happiness. While the truly religious man is able to look at things in this light, the man without Dharma, as we said above, having no knowledge of cause and effect, grieves and laments when he comes to unsatisfactory feelings, and so intensifies his duhkha. Hence he has no opportunity to experience the real happiness of Dharma.

The human personality comprises both the physical body and the various processes mental and emotional which are collectively called 'mind' or citta. Of these two, mind is the principal.[6] Since mind is the ruler of

Avalokitesvara – the Bodhisattva of Compassion. Statue at Thekchen Choling, Dharmsala, India

the body, it is obvious that bodily experience, pleasant or painful, to a great extent depends upon the mind. Turning aside from the path of Dharma, one is liable to experience much suffering. For instance, some desire the pleasures of the wealthy so they exert themselves to gain more money. From the very beginning they will be stricken with worries thinking that after their greatest efforts, both mental and physical, even then it may not be possible for them to fulfill their cherished desires. To fulfill them, they are ready to undergo any kind of suffering. Certainly, they will suffer insecurity, fearing that they may be robbed of their wealth, lose it in some way, waste and exhaust it in some fashion, and so on, and this is just another form of duhkha or suffering. Hence they search for ways to protect their gains which, since they may conflict with the interests of others, give rise to loss of harmony in society and warring factions. These in turn stir up more greed and hatred ensuring that these qualities become even stronger in the hearts of those without Dharma. Even to the richest man death comes at last and his jealously guarded wealth becomes the property of others. Such sufferings which usually go hand in hand with wealth come about from a lack of proper understanding regarding Dharma. If Dharma is deeply penetrated, one will regard the wealth one has acquired as drops of dew upon the tips of grass-blades, and so give up the unending struggle to gain more and more of it. Then, if one has to part with it, from whatever cause, one will not suffer.[7]

Likewise, even if abused or bitterly criticized, one will not suffer in one's heart so long as one is not attached to name and fame. Such conduct on the part of others will then have as little result as speech affects a stone, or be as meaningless as echoes. The detached man has no life-long enemies to overcome, nor anxiety lest he fail to favor relatives or those in authority, nor yet the anguish of defeat. None of the eight worldly conditions (lokadharma)—gain, loss, dishonor, honor, blame, praise and happiness or misery—can ruffle such a man; but should one become upset over these matters then this is due to lack of understanding regarding Dharma, or because even if one has understood Dharma, one has not put it into real practice.

The quintessence of Dharma indeed reveals that the power of these means for gaining sensual pleasures is no greater than that of a dewdrop upon a blade of grass before the sun rises. This assertion made in the Dharma is not imaginary, it is not a supposition, it is a fact to be observed in one's own and others' lives. An experience to be understood should be viewed together with the conditions which preceded it. This is the scientific way of Dharma which thus shows us how to view causes and effects. The insubstantiality of the means to sensual enjoyment is uncovered when an analysis of the factors involved is made but people do not understand this easily. When one does come to understand how pleasures are gained at a great cost, how insecure is their enjoyment, how they arise due to a complex of conditions, and how unstable and fleeting is their nature, then because one sees the need for Dharma, one's life is greatly changed. The pursuit of pleasure out of which arose lust, hatred, attraction and attachment, is changed to the pursuit of Dharma. Those mental stains formerly so difficult to control being the dominant forces in a mind ignorant of Dharma, become weakened as their causes are understood. When the way of Dharma is known and the mind thoroughly established upon it, then one has the capacity to withstand the attacks of those mental stains (kleśa) by such means as forbearance, self-restraint or mental discrimination,[8] then one should make an effort to be completely free from them.

The Dharma encourages man to understand that he can be free from all the varied hardships of duḥkha, whether internal or external, and can also lessen the storm of suffering which rages among other human beings.

From ignorance of Dharma there comes into existence the following succession of events: a continuous stream of enemies in ever-increasing numbers, the rivalry from achieving selfish aims, the effort to defeat others in this struggle while one triumphs as the conqueror. Those who view the world in this way try to make their own nation powerful and for this they equip their forces with the most deadly weapons, and then, no longer able to arrive at a peaceful settlement of disputes, prepare for terrible wars. Because of these uncontrolled stains in the hearts of individuals, the strong currents of lust, hatred, delusion, anger, greed, conceit, cruelty and violence and so on, begin to rush along with full force like the roaring of mighty rivers carrying all before them. The result of all this, for beings who have no refuge, is that they are compelled against their wishes to exist amidst these torrents of duhkha; while, if only men had an understanding of Dharma and were guided by it, then this tumult of various sufferings would cease.

As remarked upon in the paragraphs above, human life is dominated by the mind and its various functions. Thus, 'I-making,' jealousy, lust, hatred, and delusion all arise out of the mind's workings and because they are harmful both to oneself and to others, they are called unskillful dharmas (mental events). Likewise friendliness, kindness, service, devotion, renunciation and trust are also mental events but these, due to their beneficial nature are called skillful dharmas (kuśala-dharma). By the power of such skillful dharmas, the faults and stains present in the mind can be neutralized and it is just these dharmas which, if intentionally cultivated, can save a man from being drowned in his own faults. Salvation from the stains of one's own mind is greatly aided if moral shame (hrī) is developed since this causes one to esteem highly such qualities as friendliness, compassion and mutual gladness (maitrī, karuṇā, muditā). Fear of blame (anapatrapā) by others also helps since it prevents one from indulgence in unlawful and immoral actions. These two virtues are indeed like watchmen which guard a man against the commission of evil.[9] Because of their effectiveness, one is safe from many kinds of carelessness in wrong-doing, thus coming to live life contentedly. In the life of one content, there is happiness and peace and he never feels his life too difficult to bear.

It is for the above reasons that one should understand the quintessence of Dharma and apply it thoroughly in one's life.

REBIRTH[10]

(*Punarbhāva*)

ANOTHER point should also be considered: that the present life of man is not the end of everything. One does not arrive at the end of one's duty by merely making this life comfortable. The future of repeated birth stretches before one and its course may be long. That path which one will have to follow may lead through many births and, to ensure that they are happy and free from duhkha, we have to consider what skillful means may be adopted. Ultimately, of course, our aim is to find freedom from this continuity of worldly happiness and duhkha by the experience of the highest peace or happiness, which is Nirvāṇa.

Therefore, it is well to repeat that to be set merely upon gaining happiness and prosperity here in this life is certainly neither a worthy nor sufficient aim. When this life ceases, that happiness and wealth so laboriously contrived also ceases, but the mind-continuum flows on experiencing birth in a new life according to the fruits of karma. By skillful deeds here and now, these future lives become endowed with happiness-producing conditions. This skillful work, of which the fruits are to be reaped in the future, can only be accomplished by practicing Dharma.

Now, those who are ignorant of the Dharma and those who do not understand its depths, cherish doubts about rebirth. They may suppose that the consciousness which in this life is partly dependent upon the physical body, is really totally derived from it, arising with it and therefore utterly ceasing with it. They also assume that this present life has no connection to past existences. This is thought to be the truth because of another assumption: that because the events of this life are perceived and remembered, so those of past lives should also be perceived by means of the memory. Further, they have not seen or experienced with their own eyes the existence of past or future lives. Thus they declare that at death the body reverts to the four great elementals[11] while consciousness disappears as a rainbow in the sky. People of this sort have a view which is limited, for while they see the dependence of mental continuity upon the physical body, they do not understand that the mind can also be independent of a gross physical base.

The essence of the above statements from a philosophical point of view is that consciousness in this life springs out of a collection of unconscious inorganic elements. Thus the nature of the supposed cause (unconscious elements) differs from that of the supposed effect (conscious mind) and this agrees with some materialists' views since they aver that cause and effect must differ: just as from a magnifying glass, fire is produced, or from wine comes intoxication.

Further, there are logicians of the "spontaneous production school"[12] who say that the arising of things is without cause. Who has made the sharpness of the thorn, or the iridescent colors on the peacock's tail? Who has seen the Creator of such as these? Then, as to the practices of non-violence or giving, has anyone with certainty seen the results of these actions? Do we not find misers who are rich and murderers who live long? So these logicians say and argue from such examples that it will not be proper to suppose any relationships of cause and effect.

In time past, some teachers (outside Buddhadharma) affirmed that through the power of their super knowledge (abhijñā), they saw that a man miserly in his former birth, had been reborn in a prosperous family.[13] On the basis of their vision they held that the theory of rebirth was correct but that it is not proper to establish a relationship of cause-and-effect between past lives and the present one.

Others who practiced meditation, after having established themselves in the highest realms of form and formlessness (rūpāvacara, arūpāvacara), supposed that they had attained the freedom of Nirvāṇa. Although they convinced themselves that they were freed, after falling away from the power of those absorptions (dhyāna), they found themselves, nevertheless, still subject to rebirth. On the grounds of their experience, they rejected teachings which spoke of a permanent freedom, declaring themselves that such freedom did not exist.[14]

Now after presenting these various wrong views which cluster about the teachings on rebirth, we should make it clear that there are very strong arguments in favor of rebirth whereby its truth is established almost without question. We should consider this subject in the following way: any knowledge which arises in the mind, arises depending upon the succession of previous mental states (in the same series, meaning the continuum of " minds " which constitute a mind). It is clear from ordinary everyday knowledge that a man of any age, whether boy, youth or aged man, remembers past events which have taken place in his present life. His present experiences are in fact based upon the knowledge he collected previously. Life is in fact a stream of such knowledge and prior experience results in later knowledge. It can be seen clearly that no knowledge arises without a previous cause and that there is no cause for the arising and comprehending of knowledge which is external (to one's own continuity since only in one's own mental continuum can be stored the knowledge gained from one's own experience. One's own mind thus becomes the basis for future understanding).

Again, knowledge does not arise from material sources since these are of a nature different from the mind. On the contrary, after arising from causes of a non-material nature, knowledge appears to us having just this same non-material nature and this is what we call the present life. Every mental state arises dependent upon another mental state.[15]

Life is not only a collection of material causes and substances but is a series of mental events and that mentality arises from previous minds of a like nature. For this reason, neither is the present life without cause, nor has it an eternal cause, nor is it caused by mere materiality.[16] When one says that life is the stream of mental states (citta) of the same nature, this means that the present mental state both resembles and depends upon past mental states of the same nature. This is what is meant by a like born-from-like philosophy.

Mind is luminous, it is radiant,[17] it is actually knowledge itself. For this reason, the cause of knowledge is not of a different nature. If it were so, with the development or decline of the body, the mind would necessarily be subject to the same processes. Further, mind could appear in a corpse (since according to materialist views, mind is but a function of the elements). It is quite correct to state that there is a relationship between mind and body, but knowing this should not lead one to think that mind springs from the body. Likewise, it is correct to say that development and decline of the mind depends to some extent upon this physical body but even so the body cannot be called the material base for the mind. The body is only the co-operating cause for the mind since a material object can never be a cause of mind. Materiality (rūpa), is devoid of mind or citta which is mentality (nāma). That which is not mind cannot become mind, neither mind become non-mind because the nature of mind and the nature of non-mind differ from each other. Some (outsiders) insist that such change is possible and they cite examples from the changes in material things.[18] They also say that form may become formless, or in reverse process, that arūpa may develop into rūpa. The formless (arūpa) mental states are compared to space but as everyone knows, non-space cannot become space, nor what is space turn into non-space.

The material cause of the body consisting of the sperm of man and the egg-cell of woman, cannot be a (material) cause for the childs' mind as well, only for his body. We know also that knowledge possessed by a father cannot transmigrate to his child and so it becomes easy to understand that just as the material elements from the parents cannot be the cause of the child's mind, so neither can the minds of mother and father be its cause. If it were possible that the knowledge possessed by parents could be transmitted to their children, then a foolish child could not be born of an intelligent mother and father. But the truth of the matter is that the mind of the past life is the cause for the mind in the present one. There is no doubt of course, that the body is derived from the union of the sperm with the egg-cell.

There arises a question at this point. When the relationship between mind and body is not material cause and what is derived from material cause, then what is the relationship? The answer lies in karma, or the power of intentional actions, which brings about this connection. We see that newly born children or calves know how to suck milk and later become able to feed themselves and show tendencies to greed and anger, yet where did they acquire these knowledges and tendencies? This inborn knowledge can only be accounted for as the karma-fruits of a previous life since it is this which has established the connection between body and mind in the present one.

It is not proper to think that there are no past and future lives just because one has not seen them. The non-perception of something does not prove its non-existence. This is well illustrated in the present time when, with the aid of modern instruments, many facts are known and many things seen which were unknown to our forefathers. Now, the existence of past lives has been confirmed by those practicing collectedness (samādhi).[19] They, having become absorbed in high levels of mind-concentration when the mind is very subtle, and able to perceive very subtle objects, have experienced their previous births. Some meditators of great experience have recalled even in great detail, many previous lives. Even without taking into account the evidence supplied by such masters of deep meditation, there have been and are found at the present time, many incidents illustrating rebirth, from many countries in the world. From time to time small children talk about their work in a previous life and can name the family in which they lived. Sometimes it is possible to check such cases and so prove that the facts remembered by the child are not at all nonsense but are indeed true.

As an instance of this, there is the account of a Buddhist scholar in India who had to prove rebirth to an opponent convinced of the truth of Lokāyata doctrines (Materialism). In the debate with his opponent which was held before the king, the Buddhist scholar undertook to prove in a practical way that rebirth was a true doctrine. Just there, in the presence of that king, he gave up his life voluntarily, asking that monarch to be the witness of his death and of his promise to be reborn. The rival Lokāyatas after his demise became so strong that no one dared speak against their teachings. The king then published an open invitation to any Buddhist who could prove the truth of rebirth. No one offered any reply except a boy of four or five years old who, to the surprise of his mother, said that he could prove rebirth. Going before that king, he reminded him of the previous events that had occurred and stated that he was formerly the Buddhist scholar. This boy later became very famous as a Buddhist poet, the works of Chandragomin, for that was his name, being well known to scholars for their poetic excellence. In Tibet likewise, there have been many who could give detailed information about their personal belongings and the people associated with them in their past lives.

Since the karma made by us in the present will certainly lead to the experience of future lives, we should prepare for them now. How can we do so?

By aiming at a mind free from mental defilement or stains (kleśa) while acquiring virtues. This can be done only by right understanding (of what constitutes unskill and mental stains on the one hand, and what is skilled conduct or merit on the other). For this we must direct the course taken by the stream of mind and this again involves right understanding. It is only possible to dry up the stream of water which is the mind flowing through birth and death by practicing in the correct way and this may need many lives. Or, one can stop the torrent of the stream in this very life by applying oneself to the practice of the most profound skillful-means.[20]

For the ending of the wandering-on, we are concerned with the following three points:

The Dual Truth which should be analyzed and thoroughly understood.

The Dual Path of *Wisdom* and *Skillful Means* to be adopted as one's path of practice.

And based upon this, one should know the secret of achieving the *Threefold Body* which constitutes the final goal.

These three important points should be explained in due order.

THE TWO LEVELS OF TRUTH

(*Paramartha-Satya; Samvṛti-Satya*)

ALL objects known to us (through the five senses plus mind, the sixth) are divided into two categories: Those which are relatively true (samvṛti-satya) and those absolutely true (paramartha-satya). Things which are totally untrue actually do not exist, nor are they objects of knowledge. It is for this reason that objects of knowledge, in whatever way perceived, are designated by the term "truth" (satya, literally "is-ness"). Two levels or aspects of truth have been distinguished because they are quite different from one another. Any perceptible object which is true from the Absolute point of view, is bound to be viewed differently from the relative view-point. The conventional or relative truth of an object is its supposed existence while its existence from the Absolute point of view cannot therefore accord with this conventional truth. It is therefore said that these two levels of truth are mutually exclusive.

Although it may not seem proper to term both of these opposing points, " truth " yet for the sake of including all perceptible objects, they are called " true," no matter on which level they are perceived. In fact, truth is one[21] and that is Absolute Truth. If this did not exist, relative truth would have no meaning. Apart from these two levels of truth there is no third which could stand between them.

In order to understand the secret of these two levels of truth, we must pay attention to the characteristics of both, when it will then become clear that they are inseparable. While it has just been pointed out that these two are contrary to one another, this does not conflict with the statement that the nature of both is basically the same. If in fact *they are not of the same nature and are held to be of different natures*, then many fallacies may be found, of which we here discern four:

1. If they are of different natures, then a material object may be held to be really substantial (since absolutely, insubstantiality is taught). It will then mean that the ultimate nature of an object has nothing whatsoever to do with its attributes (arising from its supposed essence). In this case, people will never know that the existence of objects or their supposed essence, is truly the insubstantial, the void, the not-self, and even the knowledge which would reveal this to them must remain a secret.

2. Again, when different natures for the two levels of truth are propounded, even if people know that objects are insubstantial and so on, they can never

penetrate to the real nature of relative truth (and so destroy delusion) since it seems to turn relative into an absolute truth.

3. It follows that it will be useless for meditators to train themselves in the way of the absorptions (dhyāna) and so forth, having the idea that thereby they may realize " non-self-nature " (niḥsvabhāvatā) because if the Absolute Truth is independent of the relative, then attainment-knowledge in the meditator will be obstructed by the meditation-object (which is relative) and by his attachment to it. As a result, the knowledge which is unobstructed, detached and objectless will not arise in him and thus perfection and even knowledge of the Way will be hard to obtain.

4. If such is the case, then one may say that Lord Buddha's understanding was not free from clinging to objects and to their self-nature (svabhāva) so that the subtle stains connected with this were not uprooted by him.

On the other hand, *if the two truths do not differ at all* then four further faults may be discerned:

1. By ceasing to distinguish the illusory, relative truth involving karma (intentional action) and the mental stains, we must also cease to distinguish the Absolute Truth (of Nirvāṇa).

2. If this assumption was true, as relative dharmas (events) are various, some being imperceptible, then absolute dharmas would also have to be many and imperceptible, while it is a fact that Absolute Truth is one and not impossible to perceive (since perception

of it is had by the Buddhas or Arahats who have experienced Nirvāṇa).

3. A fallacy is also committed in this assumption by an ordinary-man (pṛthagjana) who while overpowered by ignorance (avidyā), thinks that he has discarded the mental stains (kleśa) and has realized Buddhahood. If this were so, then there could be no attainment as a Noble Person (āryapudgala), Stream-enterer up to Arhat).

4. The most important fault would be that as dharmas are relatively true and therefore full of deficiencies, so the Absolute Truth would be likewise[22] (but Nirvāṇa is perfection).

The apparent contradictions between these two levels of truth should be resolved by explaining that although by nature (svabhāva) they are not different, yet for practical purposes they are so.

Absolute Truth is that which is realized by deep reasoning and contemplating the absolute or true nature of dharmas, while the dharmas which are given a name and cognized by the mind as such, are called relative truth. To understand this more clearly, let us take the help of etymology and examine the terms Paramartha-Satya and Samvṛti-Satya. In the first of these, "parama" means "excellent, best, supreme, highest," while the word "artha" here signifies "that which it is able" (to know with the highest wisdom). It may also mean "that which can be examined by the highest wisdom." A knowable dharma such as this is called "paramartha" because it is the most excellent, indeed supreme, among all dharmas to be known. Literally, the word "satya" means "is-ness" or "things-as-they-are" and if we think carefully about it, to whatever "is-ness" applies, *that* cannot be otherwise and must therefore be permanent and hence is called Absolute Truth.

Samvṛti-Satya means the view that grasps the truth of the real nature of the dharmas.[23] It is called samvṛti or relative because what is perceived from the angle of this truth is relatively true; or its meaning may be taken as "wrong, false" because the way that an object appears in the light of this truth is really distorted, there being no unity between the relative perception of the object and its essential nature. Although ultimately this "truth" is false yet the appearances created in a mind governed by relative truth are to that extent true, hence we say that it is "satya."

For a better understanding of Absolute Truth, we may analyze it as follows:

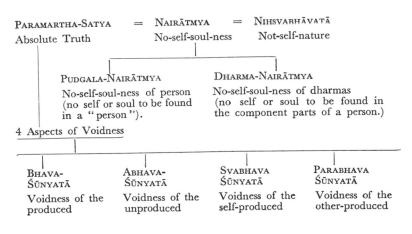

PARAMARTHA-SATYA = NAIRĀTMYA = NIHSVABHĀVATĀ
Absolute Truth — No-self-soul-ness — Not-self-nature

- PUDGALA-NAIRĀTMYA
  No-self-soul-ness of person (no self or soul to be found in a "person").
- DHARMA-NAIRĀTMYA
  No-self-soul-ness of dharmas (no self or soul to be found in the component parts of a person.)

4 Aspects of Voidness

- BHAVA-ŚŪNYATĀ
  Voidness of the produced
- ABHAVA-ŚŪNYATĀ
  Voidness of the unproduced
- SVABHAVA ŚŪNYATĀ
  Voidness of the self-produced
- PARABHAVA ŚŪNYATĀ
  Voidness of the other-produced

These classifications may be further elaborated into sixteen, eighteen or twenty aspects of voidness but the above four aspects will suffice for our present purpose.[24] This is only intended as a preliminary clarification of what is meant by Absolute Truth, while a full account of no-self-soul-ness (anātmatā) will be found in the section on the "Training in Supreme Wisdom."

THE HEAPS, ENTRANCES AND ELEMENTS

(skandha, āyatana, dhātu)

ALL dharmas except voidness are included under the heading of relative truth which thus covers the classifications known as the five Heaps (skandha), the twelve Entrances (āyatana) and the eighteen Elements (dhātu). Skandha means heap, group, collection or aggregate, the five Heaps moreover being interdependent and born or arising together. The Āyatana or Entrances are the sources for the arising of mind and the mental-events (citta, caittadharma). The Dhātu are the origin (ākara) and within these eighteen classes can be placed all objects in the world.

THE FIVE HEAPS

1. The form-heap (rūpa-skandha) is elevenfold comprising the five subjective sense-bases plus the five outer objects:

Eye-Base	Ear-Base	Nose-Base	Tongue-Base	Body-Base
↕	↕	↕	↕	↕
Visibles	Audibles	Smellables	Gustibles	Touchables

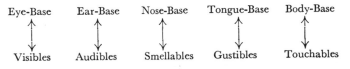

The eleventh constituent is the form which is not perceptible (avijñaptirūpa).[25]

2. The feeling-heap (vedanā-skandha) consists of the three sorts of feelings: pleasant, unpleasant, and those which are neither.

3. Saṃjñā-skandha, or the cognition-heap (including memory) includes these two divisions: svavicāra and avicāra, recollection of cognition and absence of recollection of it, while each of these two are sub-divided into: limited, extensive, and infinite.

4. Saṃskāra-skandha or the heap of volitional formations contains the mental-coefficients variously classified into those associated with consciousness (samprayukta caitta-dharma), and the rest dissociated from consciousness (viprayukta caitta-dharma).[26]

5. The last of the five heaps is that of consciousness (vijñāna-skandha) in which are found the six types of consciousness, each one of which is connected to the appropriate one of the six sense-bases. From these six types of consciousness there is general knowledge of objects.

THE TWELVE ENTRANCES

are as follows:

	Ten Material Entrances					2 Mental Entrances
Subjective	Eye Entrance	Ear Entrance	Nose Entrance	Tongue Entrance	Body Entrance	Mind Entrance
Objective	Form Entrance	Sound Entrance	Smell Entrance	Taste Entrance	Touch Entrance	Mental Event Entrance

Though the eye-dominant (cakṣendriya) and the eye-entrance here have the same connotation, as form-heap and form (rūpa), there is a difference of connotation between form and the form-entrance here, since the former includes all the eleven categories of form while the latter is only that form which is the object of the eye-dominant (or eye-entrance) in terms of colors and forms.

The ear-dominant (śrotendriya) and the ear-entrance here, also have the same connotation, so that what has been said above should be applied to every one of these entrances.

As we may see from the above table, the entrances are divided, for the purpose of analysis, into subjective and objective, as well as into material and mental. Citta (heart, mind), manas (mind, thought) and vijñāna (consciousness) have all the same connotation for which reason all mental states such as eye-consciousness, are included under the mind-entrance here. Space (ākāśa, śūnyatā) and all other unconditioned dharmas are placed in the mental-event entrance.

THE EIGHTEEN ELEMENTS

are classified thus:

Dominant Elements	Eye Element	Ear Element	Nose Element	Tongue Element	Body Element	Mind Element
Object Elements	Form Element	Sound Element	Smell Element	Taste Element	Touch Element	Mental Event Element
Consciousness Elements	Eye-Consciousness Element	Ear-Consciousness Element	Nose-Consciousness Element	Tongue-Consciousness Element	Body-Consciousness Element	Mind-Consciousness Element

The above table shows the eighteen elements distributed amongst the three categories of dominant, object and consciousness elements. The dominants (indriya), that is the various sense faculties, which are the sources of the respective consciousnesses, are called the dominant elements (indriya-dhātu), the six types of consciousness which arise in dependence upon the respective six dominants are called the consciousness-elements (vijñāna-dhātu) while the six objects such as form, sound, and so on, which are the objects of these six consciousnesses, are known as the six object-elements (viṣaya-dhātu).

Briefly, all conditioned dharmas are included in the five heaps. The twelve entrances include both conditioned and unconditioned dharmas. Again, all knowable dharmas are included in the eighteen element classification. All the objects of knowledge which we spoke of in the section on two levels of truth, are included both in the twelve entrances and among the eighteen elements. When these eighteen elements are analyzed in detail, sixty-two components may be discerned and to have right understanding of them, it is indispensable to know their nature, function, category and so forth, together with knowledge of which among them is to be abandoned, and which it is proper to develop. Fearing that this book may become too long, this information is not included here and readers are advised to consult more specialized treatises.

It is the duty of a good Buddhist to gain right understanding of these heaps, entrances and elements, so that he can in his own experience, discriminate quickly, and accurately, observing to himself, "O this is such and such a heap, entrance" just as these arise. This analytic knowledge (for use in daily life as an adjunct of the insight or vipaśyanā—Pali: vipassanā—meditations) coupled with the understanding of abandoning and development, helps one to attain the supreme peace (Nirvāṇa).

Much against his wishes each man is wandering in the cycle of unsatisfactory experience, or duhkha, also called the wheel of birth-and-death, whereby he comes to suffer in very many different ways. The causes of this ever-present cycle of duhkha are collectively the stains or defilement of mind (kleśa) such as greed, aversion and delusion. As these have deep roots in the mind of man, until and unless *one annihilates them completely, it is not possible to dry up the stream of duhkha.* To achieve freedom from duhkha and to attain that release which is great peace and sublime happiness, there is one and only one means, that is, by the destruction of these stains of greed, aversion and delusion which are inborn in our minds. How this may be accomplished will be outlined in the following sections of this book.

THE THREE COLLECTIONS OF BUDDHA-WORD

(*Tripiṭaka*)

LORD Buddha has taught all the 84,000 sections of Dharma (into which the whole teaching may be divided) just for the purpose of instructing people in the means whereby they may destroy the mental stains and so experience supreme peace. Only by practicing the methods of Dharma taught in these 84,000 sections can these stains be rid off. A briefer classification of the teaching is the twelvefold teaching of Dharma,[27] while if a still briefer division is adopted, then all Lord Buddha's teachings are said to be contained within the three collections (literally " baskets ").

These are: the Collection of Discipline (*Vinaya Piṭaka*), of Discourses (*Sūtra Piṭaka*) and of the pragmatic psychoethical philosophy called the *Abhidharma Piṭaka*. The compilers of these three collections (who were the great bhikṣus of the first and second councils) have arranged the great mass of Lord Buddha's teachings into these three categories for various reasons. Nine of these which are among the most important have been selected for explanation here. Of these nine, three explaining respectively Sūtra, Vinaya and Abhidharma are from the viewpoint of *those dharmas to be destroyed.* A further three are concerned with *those dharmas which should be developed*, or the three collections from the point of view of the training, while the last are the Sūtra, Vinaya and Abhidharma viewed from the angle of *those dharmas which should be known.* We have thus a sequence of destruction (of the unskillful), development (of the skillful), and knowledge or realization (of the truth) which must be the order followed by everyone who wishes to practice the Dharma.

Three Reasons from the Viewpoint of Destruction

Corresponding to the three collections are three mental stains showing the respective functions of these collections. These three stains obstruct the way to freedom so that those people who desire to experience freedom, must destroy them.

The first of these stains is *scepticism* (vicikitsa) which creates doubt in the minds of men regarding the truth of the Four Noble Truths and Dependent Arising.[28] By pondering over the Collection of Discourses one can get rid of scepticism, since the contents of this collection may be verified and thus seen as opposed to this stain. Why is this so? In the Collection of Discourses the individual and general characteristics [29] of the heaps, entrances and elements, dependent origination, the Four Noble Truths, the ten levels, ten perfecting qualities and many others, are clearly shown while the supreme training in collectedness is vividly clarified. By making plain these two characteristics, one may become free of scepticism when it is possible to arrive at a sure understanding. The nature of scepticism, however, is that it does not allow this to happen, keeping the mind in vacillation between all sorts of extremes and opposites. It is therefore said that the *Sūtra Piṭaka* has been taught to counteract this stain of scepticism.[30]

Such extremes as indulgence in sense-pleasures on the one hand, or torture of the body by vows of asceticism with the idea of purifying the mind on the other, should be avoided, and to overcome them Lord Buddha has taught the Middle Path of Practice.[31] Now the second of the obstructing stains causes *attachment to extreme views* (antadvayānuyojaka). By pondering over the *Vinaya Piṭaka* this stain can be destroyed so that it is said of the Discipline that it stands opposed to the extreme-views-attachment. How is this so? The detailed analysis of conduct found in the Discipline Collection shows the faults of indulgence in sensual pleasures, such as rich food, comfortable soft beds, sexual intercourse,[32] and so on, and thus encourages people to check themselves. The two extremes mentioned above are called being drowned in sense-pleasures (kāmeṣu-kāma-sukhallikānuyoga) and its opposite, the practice of bodily torture to gain self-purification (ātmaklamathānuyoga), so it is quite clear that restraint (saṃvara) as taught in the *Vinaya Piṭaka* will oppose this stain.

Although the contents of the Discipline Collection have been emphasized as opposed to indulgence in sense-pleasures, yet for those who are possessed of pure virtue and non-attachment and who moreover, without effort gain both respect and materials for their comfort (due to their merits) and are able to check their attachments to such things, for them, Lord Buddha has allowed the acceptance of fine foods and the rest. As he has not approved of strict austerity for all indiscriminately, this part of his teaching in the *Vinaya Piṭaka* stands opposed to the extreme of self-torture. The essence of this matter may be summed up thus: a person who possesses much and uses it without being attached, remaining unstained by passion, is indeed of pure character and fit to possess wealth and fame, etc.; while a bhikṣu who uses only three robes stitching these from rags collected off a rubbish heap (paṃsakūlacīvara) yet has attachment for them, is of stained character and is not permitted by Lord Buddha to accept the extra allowances. Allowance and prohibition in the practice of vinaya depend upon the decrease or increase respectively, of the mental stains and not upon the mere requisites (or possessions) themselves. Hence, the *Vinaya Piṭaka* has been taught to counteract the stain dragging one to hold tightly to extreme views.

Now we come to consider the third mental stain which is the dogmatic view declaring: "my own view is the truth and all others are wrong." One may grasp at such a view so strongly that one never wishes to relinquish it. This is called "idam-satyābhiniveṣa"[33] or literally, "*this-is-truth-dogmatic-belief*" and is the third stain to be abandoned here. How can this be done? By pondering over the *Abhidharma Piṭaka* which is thus said to be opposed to such dogmatic views.

Study of the Abhidharma by listening, reading and reflection results in clear understanding of the individual and general characteristics [34] of the three marks of impermanence, unsatisfactoriness and not-self-soul. Since people do not have insight regarding these three marks, they fall into the pit of wrong views and so, pervertedly, mistake the unsatisfactory for happiness, perceive the impermanent as permanent, think of a self-soul entity in what is devoid of such, and lastly, see the unbeautiful as beautiful. Holding such perverted views they may go on to regard wrong standards of moral conduct as the right standards and what is in fact unskillful practice as skillful practice. The Abhidharma shows clearly the characteristics of the dharmas and their effects and so helps establish right understanding which itself is opposed to all wrong views leading one astray, among which is found the dogmatic view: "This is truth, all else is false." It is said that the Abhidharma was taught for the purpose of destroying such wrong views while upholding the supremacy of the Buddha's path of practice.

Three Reasons from the Viewpoint of Training

All Lord Buddha's instruction may be summarized under the headings of the threefold training: Virtue (śīla), Collectedness (samādhi) and Wisdom (prajñā) for which see the following section.

Referring to the three collections of Buddha-word, firstly, in the *Sūtras* or Discourses all of the training in each of the three aspects is described. Now from the Śrāvakayāna[35] point of view, virtue consists of the Prātimokṣa precepts (see below), guarding oneself against straying from the field of righteous conduct and care lest one commit the slightest fault thus staining one's purity. Being able to dwell in the attainments of absorption (dhyāna) and in the formless spheres (arūpa-samāpatti) constitutes the training in collectedness, while insight (vipaśyanā) into the Four Noble Truths is the training in wisdom.

From the Mahāyāna viewpoint, the training in virtue is the extinction of all wrong conduct,[36] while that of collectedness is seen in the attainment of the two types of practice known as Gaganagañja and Śūraṃgama.[37] The wisdom-training is then the experience of non-discriminating knowledge (nirvikalpa-jñāna) regarding the dharmas, which is knowing based on Absolute Truth. In this way both in Śrāvakayāna and in Mahāyāna Discourse Collections, the whole of the threefold training is taught.

Coming now to the *Vinaya Piṭaka*, or Collection of Discipline, it is said that here both virtue and collectedness are taught. Since the Discipline informs one what should be avoided and what may be accepted, one's virtue becomes purified. Due to this purification, disturbance and remorse cannot arise in the mind. When the mind is not disturbed, this results in lightness of the body and its easy workability. With tranquility of mind comes the suffusion of joy and happiness throughout both mind and body. When this is experienced, a meditator establishes one-pointedness and so is able to enter a state of collectedness (samādhi).[38] It is in this way that *Vinaya* teaches both the trainings of virtue and of collectedness.

The third collection is that of the Abhidharma in which wisdom alone is taught. In this collection a thorough analysis is made to ascertain the natures of all the dharmas. By listening, reading and reflecting, wisdom arises free from delusion which penetrates to the nature of the dharmas. Thus does the *Abhidharma Piṭaka* instruct one in the wisdom-training.

Three Reasons from the Viewpoint of Knowledge

The Discourse Collection contains both the literal meaning (vyañjana) of the Dharma and the explained or expanded meaning conveyed thereby (artha). Here literal Dharma means the letters, words and terms used in the teaching such as "heaps," "entrances," or "elements," while the information derived from the use of these terms is the expanded or essential meaning. There is another way of exposition for it is said that heaps, entrances and elements are the literal Dharma while the fourfold method of conveying meaning and the fourfold relationships are the explained or essential meaning. Again, we may say that literal Dharma

His Holiness Tenzin Gyatsho, The XIVth Dalai Lama of Tibet.
Photograph by John Faber

The Potala, traditional residence of the Dalai Lamas at Lhasa in Tibet. Construction was commenced by the Fifth Dalai Lama about 1645 A.D. This is a tapestry portrait.

means the way of the ten skillful deeds (see next section, on virtue) leading to experience of celestial states, while the Practice-path consisting of the thirty-seven Wings of Enlightenment leading to Nirvāṇa is the essential meaning. In this way the Discourse Collection gives the correct meanings of both the literal and the explained meanings.

Next come the *Vinaya* which shows the dharmas to be developed and those to be destroyed so that one who practices is established in pure virtue (the literal sense), while as it also encourages the practice of meditating on the foul (aśubha-bhāvanā) and so on, there is the destruction of the mental stains (the essential meaning). Thus, when a man is possessed of pure virtue, his mental stains may be destroyed so that these two aspects of the teaching, vyañjana and artha, appear in his continuity. In this way the *Vinaya* gives confirmation of both aspects of the Dharma to one who practices it.

Study of the *Abhidharma* gives men the ability to express in words for others' benefit, the literal and the expanded meanings of Dharma.

The categories described above show the reasons respectively why the *Sūtra*, *Vinaya* and *Abhidharma* Collections were taught and how they accord on various levels with destruction, training and knowledge, thus illustrating the synthesis of skillful-means and wisdom to be seen in the whole Buddhist teaching and in all three vehicles—that of disciples, of Silent Buddhas, and of the Great Vehicle.[39]

THE THREEFOLD TRAINING

(*Triśikṣā*)

THE whole of Lord Buddha's teaching can be summarized under the headings of adhiśīla, adhisamādhi and adhiprajñā since all the topics discussed in the three Collections fall under one or other of these headings. In each of these three terms, "*adhi*" as a prefix signifies "special" or "supreme." Thus the term "adhisīla" means "special" or "supreme virtue." It is called "special," etc. because it proves to be a benefit both to him who observes it as well as to others both in the present and in future lives. The standards of virtue held by those of other views (non-Buddhists) is not of this category. For instance, ritualistic views, as in Hindu practice, hold that it is virtuous to perform the austerity of the "fivefold fire," which in fact can never be either for one's own benefit nor for that of others but rather is liable to give trouble to all concerned.[40] Since, on the contrary, both oneself and others profit from the training in supreme virtue, it is rightly acclaimed the highest.

Similarly, one may see why the training in supreme collectedness (adhisamādhi-śikṣā) is so called. Thus collectedness as one may ascertain by practice, opposes mental stains and the indulgence in evil thoughts thus leading not only to happiness in future lives but also to happiness here-and-now. Nor is that all. Eventually, by the practice of collectedness taught in the Buddhadharma, one may experience the supermundane bliss of Nirvāṇa. For this reason, the collectedness taught by Lord Buddha cannot be labelled " ordinary " but is said to be " special " or " supreme." The samādhi taught by outsiders only has the effect of calming the mind, preventing its disturbance by sense-objects, hence leading to happiness here and at most to arising as a god (deva) in the celestial realms of form or formlessness (rūpārūpabhūmi) which is one of the six divisions of the wandering-on.[41] As it does not destroy the stains of the mind and its evil imaginings (since only calm [śamatha] is developed, without vipaśyanā or insight), so these samādhis of outsiders cannot be called " supreme."

In order to understand why the wisdom taught by Lord Buddha, is called Supreme Wisdom, we should know something of its scope. The belief in self or soul and the holding of the view that there is such a permanent entity, is called ātmadṛṣṭi (self-soul-view). This is divided into the two aspects of view of selfhood in the person (pudgalātmadṛṣṭi) and view of selfhood (soul) in the dharmas (dharmātmadṛṣṭi). Further, we distinguish two kinds of thought-coverings (or obstructions) called the obstruction of mental stains and the obstruction to knowledge (kleśāvaraṇa, jñeyāvaraṇa). It is the first of these which supports the view of selfhood in the person, while the second gives rise to the view of selfhood in the dharmas. It is because of these misleading views and obstructions that beings are entangled both with mental stains and with ignorance (avidyā). The wisdom taught by Lord Buddha is able to destroy those stains and obstructions for ever, for when it is put into practice and realization is won, both stains and obstructions vanish leaving unobstructed knowledge (nirāvaraṇa). Prajñā or wisdom of this type can hardly be called "ordinary" and is rightly known as Supreme Wisdom. If we examine the wisdom taught by outsiders, we shall see that it is not supreme in this way, since it does not lead to seeing-things-as-they-really-are (yathābhūtajñānadarśana) and hence not to knowledge of the Absolute Truth. This being so, it is in nowise possible to cut through the bonds of ignorance which is the root-cause of the wandering-on (saṃsāra).

I. THE TRAINING IN SUPREME VIRTUE
(Adhiśīla-śikṣā)

This is the first of the three trainings, for just as the earth is the foundation of all things in the world, so virtue is the basis and root of all skillful dharmas (kuśaladharma). All dharmas which are experienced through the practice of collectedness and wisdom, have their origin in this, the first training. While the essence of the training in supreme virtue is contained in the ten Refraining-from-Unskillful precepts, many other varieties of precepts could be described but here three will suffice:

Prātimokṣa precepts
Bodhisattva precepts } for these see below.
Vajrayāna precepts

All other groups of precepts are in fact included within the scope of these three classes. But first we shall describe the root-precepts or those ten dealing with restraint from unskill. When this type of precept is well established in a person's heart, he can guard himself even at the moment when an unskillful tendency arises in him.

TEN REFRAINING-FROM-UNSKILLFUL PRECEPTS

(daśa-akuśala-prativirati-śīla)

The ten precepts in this section are divided into three classes according to whether the action breaking them is one of body, speech or mind. The unskillful action committed by way of body are three in number, by way of speech there are four, while the remaining three are committed through the mind-door.

These unskillful actions or karma [42] as they should be called, may or may not be counted as karma-paths. Certainly those unskillful karmas which construct the way leading to the states of woe [43] are undoubtedly karma-paths. A karma to be counted as a karma-path must have the special potential to drag the person committing it, to reconnection or birth as ghost, animal or in hell. In order to be sure whether or not a karma has such potential, we must examine the factors involved in it for if these are complete, we may be sure that the karma is in fact a karma-path. Each of the ten offences below has five factors for its completion,[44] while it will be seen that restraint in respect of body, speech and mind will ensure that these offences are not committed.

1. Refraining from Destroying Life (prāṇātipāta-virati)

- i The first factor necessary to break this precept, is a living being having life other than one's own. This being which is destroyed is called the *object* (vastu).
- ii There should be the *intention* (saṃjñā) to kill knowing that it is alive.
- iii Next there must be the *effort* (prayoga) made by oneself to kill, or else the inciting of others to kill, by poison, weapons, black-magic, and so forth.
- iv To accomplish the killing, some aspect of *mental stain* (kleśa) such as greed, aversion or delusion must be present. In this case aversion (dveṣa) will often be the dominant stain.
- v The last factor is the *accomplishment* (niṣpatti) of death for a living being before the killer dies.

Only when all five of these factors are present, is killing regarded as a karma-path, for in other cases it may be only an accident or perhaps unmindful conduct although still resulting in painful consequences.

The intensity of the evil committed and the karma accumulated varies with the manner in which it was accomplished, its motive and the type of being deprived of life. Basically, killing may spring from motives based on each of the three roots of unskill: Thus, sometimes killing is done out of desire to eat an animal's flesh and where this is the case, it is accomplished by the domination of the root of greed. On other occasions, the motive for killing is anger, revenge and so forth so that the root of aversion is dominant. Where killing is performed out of wrong views such as offering animal sacrifices, the dominating root is delusion.[45] Among the many beings who may be destroyed, the killing of a religious teacher, one's mother, father, or an Arhat, or any other religious person whether a wanderer or a householder-priest, are deemed the most serious offences.

2. Refraining from Taking what is not Given (adattādāna-virati)

i The object is the wealth or property belonging to others, or that which has been dedicated to the Triple Gem.

ii The intention is desire to possess that wealth or property by means of violent robbery, stealthy removal, or else by some fraudulent dealing or cheating.

iii The effort made is either by oneself, or else by hiring or inciting others to take away what is not given.

iv All three roots among the stains may be present but among them greed will be the dominant.

v Accomplishment consists of the satisfaction in the mind of the thief which arises from his possession of the stolen article, whether or not it is removed from its place.

Taking what is not given can be accomplished in three ways: Firstly, by threatening with force a weaponless person, or by stealthy burglary and the removal of what one desires, or lastly, by various sorts of cheating and fraudulent transaction. Of all the different ways whereby this precept may be broken, the most serious is the stealing of that which is dedicated to the Triple Gem.

3. Refraining from wrong conduct in Sexual Desires (kāmamithyācāra-virati)

i The object is a member of the opposite sex with whom one should not consort, such as another's wife or husband, a woman or man in the custody of parents or guardians, or a person of the opposite sex who in taking up a religious life remains celibate. A person from a family with whom one's own has had connection in the last seven generations, is also included in the object. Under some conditions, to have intercourse even with one's own wife can constitute a breach of this precept as when it takes place near shrines or in temples, at a wrong time such as upon upavasatha (fast-day),[46] upon some inopportune occasion as during day-time, during a monthly period or else when she is pregnant, or lastly by some kind of unnatural practice through orifices other than the vagina.

ii The second factor is intention of a woman (or man) to have sexual intercourse.

iii Then there must be the effort made to accomplish this.

iv Among the various mental stains, greed is the predominant root while both of the others (aversion, delusion) may also be found.

v Accomplishment is the acceptance with delight of the feeling resulting from contact between the two sexual organs. As regards persons, this precept can be broken in three ways should sexual intercourse be had with: a woman or man supported or protected by relatives, mother, father or brother; a woman in the care of a husband (or, in the case of a man, one who is already married); thirdly, a person protected by Dharma, including all those devoting their whole lives to religious practice. Among the various sorts of sexual misconduct, the gravest would be incestuous intercourse, being an act of rape upon one's own mother who was at the same time a bhikṣunī and an Arhat.

4. Refraining from False Speech (mṛṣāvāda-virati).

i Here the object is a human being other than oneself, for there must either be someone to speak falsely to, or also about.

ii Intention is to distort the truth as for instance, when someone who has not seen, is asked and replies, "Yes, I saw . . . . . ."

iii The effort is made either through speech or by bodily action which has been preceded by considered thoughts.

iv Regarding the stains, any one of the three roots may predominate.

v Accomplishment is seen when whatever one tries to make others believe by communication of speech or body, is taken in the way intended by the liar. Expression of an untruth by words alone may be varied when bodily movements conveying untruth are used.

Three groups of offenses may be discerned here: The type of untruth told about the uttara-manuṣya-dharma, that is the laying claim to states of superhuman attainments[47] which one has not experienced, although one tries to convince others that one has done so. This is called the group leading to downfall (an inferior birth in the states of woe in future lives). Secondly, there is the lie told for the well-being of oneself and the destruction of others, and this is known as the "great falsehood."

Lastly, to lie neither for well-being nor harm, neither for oneself or others, but just from a wish to do so (perhaps in jest, etc.), is listed as a small falsehood. Of all the sorts of lies possible, the worst is to speak ill of Lord Buddha, while the deception of one's father, mother and teachers is also very serious.

5. Refraining from Slanderous Speech (paiśunyavācā-virati)

- i For object one must have at least two people who are friends.
- ii The intention is in the form of desire to destroy their friendship.
- iii While the effort consists in trying to bring about disunity.
- iv All three roots of unskill may be present among the stains but the root of aversion usually dominates.
- v In this precept, its breach is accomplished when the meanings of the words used for slander are understood by the other parties. To make effort that opposing parties do not become reconciled also comes within the scope of this precept.

Slander may be of three kinds: The first category is where forceful expression is used and the subject discussed openly, not in secret, perhaps with the pretence of sincere friendship. Slander of the second kind is effected by conveying the words of each side to the other and thus promoting disunity. Lastly, one may slander secretly and in an indirect way by using others' speech. The worst sort of slander which can possibly be effected is when the relationship between a religious teacher and his disciples is broken up, or else when the concord of a Saṃgha (community of Buddhist monks) is destroyed.

6. REFRAINING FROM HARSH SPEECH (phāruśyavācā-virati)

i As object there must be a person other than oneself to whom one speaks harshly.
ii One has already decided to speak harshly and this constitutes the intention here.
iii The effort to speak using harsh words is one's effort.
iv While all three species of mental stains may be present, the root of aversion will generally predominate.
v Finally, there is accomplishment by way of the harsh words being uttered.

There are also three sorts of speaking harshly: The first sort is when one speaks harshly face to face so that the person so addressed is humiliated. Secondly, harsh words may be aimed at another indirectly in which case he to whom the words are really addressed is hurt. The indirect way of harsh speech is seen when one gossips to the friend of the person whom one wishes to injure. This may also be done by letter. Among the various sorts of harsh speech, that addressed to an Ārya (noble one), or to mother and father, is the most serious.

7. Refraining from Foolish Chatter

(sambhinnapralāpā-virati).

i As above, the object is another person.

ii Intention is to chatter foolishly because of carelessness.

iii Effort is seen where one starts chatter, tales and useless songs.

iv While all three of the unskillful roots may be involved, the principal stain will be delusion.

v Accomplishment takes place when speech unworthy of communication issues from the mouth.

Foolish chatter is also of three sorts: Untrue nonsense, such as prayers to gods, legends, religious myths and miraculous tales; then worldly nonsense includes gossip, useless stories, fiction and jokes; while true nonsense is the teaching of Dharma to a person who is not yet ready to receive it. Considering all the types of foolish chatter, the most serious is that resulting in the mental distraction of one devoted to Dharma.

8. Refraining from Covetousness

(abhidyā-virati)

i The object here is the movable or immovable property of others.

ii Intention means to cherish wishes and hopes to possess others' property or money.
iii Effort consists of planning over and over again how that property might be acquired.
iv Of the three unskillful roots, greed predominates though the others may also be present.
v Accomplishment is seen when that planning results in the complete abandonment of shame (hrī) and fear of others' blame (apatrapā).

Covetousness is of three varieties: For property in one's own family, for others' property, or for that which does not belong to anyone. Of the sorts of covetousness possible, that for property and goods rightly held by the bhikṣusaṃgha, is the most serious.

9. Refraining from Ill-Will
(byāpāda-virati)

i A being other than oneself is the object.
ii The intention is to kill, beat or destroy others.
iii The effort made is the planning how to accomplish the harm or destruction of others.
iv While all of the unskillful roots may be present as stains, it is the root of aversion which is dominant.
v Accomplishment comes when one sees virtues in killing, beating and destroying others and no longer cares for the opposite and skillful path of friendliness and compassion (maitrī-karuṇā).

Ill-will may be divided into three categories: The thought concerned with killing others, one of sheer hatred or malice, which a soldier has upon the battlefield. Then the reflection on how one may bring harm upon another out of rivalry. Lastly, bearing enmity towards another who has wronged one even though he has subsequently apologized for his misconduct. The worst excess of ill-will is to be seen in those who contemplate the "immediacy" crimes [48] of matricide, patricide, killing an Arhat, shedding the blood of a Buddha and causing a schism in the Saṃgha.

10. Refraining from Wrong Views (mithyādṛṣṭi-virati)

i The object (vastu) are the skillful or unskillful dharmas in the mind (citta).

ii Intention (samjñā) here is to oppose cause-and-effect thinking in terms of "no dharmas are skillful, no dharmas are unskillful" and "there is no fruit either to skillful or to unskillful dharmas."

iii The effort (prayoga) made is the reflecting again and again that there are no skillful and no unskillful dharmas nor do they have any fruits.

iv Generally, delusion is strongest among the stains (kleśa) though all three of the unskillful roots may be present.

v When one is convinced of the non-existence of both skill and unskill together with the non-existence of their fruits, being thus altogether sunk in wrong views, without having any right view (or understanding) to oppose it, then there is accomplishment (niṣpatti).

Three classes of wrong views may be discerned: First, that which declares there is no karma, skillful or unskillful, and no results of karma-happiness and unsatisfactoriness (sukha, duhkha), these arising without cause. In this way the law of causation is undermined.[49] Second, the wrong view which proclaims that even though there is a path of practice and though one fullfils this practice (in Buddhist terms, the practice of the Path-truth or mārgasatya), there can be no realization (of the cessation of duhkha or nirodhasatya) thus undermining the Four Noble Truths. The third wrong view is seen in the statement that there is no Buddha or being who is enlightened by his own efforts so that there can be no Dharma (based on enlightenment) and no purpose for the Saṃgha (who are striving for enlightenment), this amounting to a thoroughly destructive criticism of the Triple Gem. Of all the different sorts of unskillful mental karma, this last false view is the most serious.

The observance of these ten precepts guarding one against the commission of the above ten unskillful karmas, is called the keeping of the Refraining-from-Unskillful Precepts, the account of which is now concluded. We should now briefly examine:

THE PRĀTIMOKṢA PRECEPTS

This word "prātimokṣa" [Pali: "pāṭimokkha"] is a compound of which the first part "*prāti*" has significance of "getting rid of," that is, of worldly duhkha, so leading those who observe these precepts to "*mokṣa*," or the freedom of Nirvāṇa.

Now, one does not keep these precepts from a desire for protection, nor from fear, nor due to desire for worldly name and fame, nor yet to gain happiness in another world; rather they are undertaken through detachment toward the whole world and with a strong desire for freedom and peace, for their practice is always accompanied by the volition of non-harming (ahimsā) toward others. Hence, they are truthfully called the precepts of Prātimokṣa.

Since there are eight classes of people who observe these precepts,[50] they are of eight kinds:

Upavasatha-śīla	(precepts kept on lunar observance days)
Upāsaka-śīla	(male devotees' precepts)
Upāsikā-śīla	(female devotees' precepts)
Śrāmaṇera-śīla	(male novices' precepts)
Śrāmaṇerikā-śīla	(female novices' precepts)
Śikṣamāṇā-śīla	(training precepts for female probationers)
Bhikṣu-śīla	(fully-ordained monks' precepts)
Bhikṣuṇī-śīla	(fully-ordained nuns' precepts)

The precepts are also known as the precepts of

restraint (samvaraśīla) and for this reason the precepts of all eight classes of persons are called collectively, the eight-personed Prātimokṣa restraint. The numbers of precepts observed by the different classes above vary thus:

> Observance-day precepts are eight in number.
> Upāsaka and Upāsikā precepts are five.
> Śramaṇera and Śramaṇerikā have each thirty-six precepts ten of which are root-precepts.[51]
> Śikṣamāṇā have twelve precepts, six of which are root-precepts to be observed two years before becoming a bhikṣuṇī.
> Bhikṣu precepts are 253 which are divided into classes with the most serious offences at the beginning, as follows:[52]
> 4 Pārājika (defeat) for the commission of these evils a bhikṣu is disrobed and cannot be re-ordained.
> 13 Saṃghāvaśeṣa (entailing an initial and subsequent meeting of the Saṃgha).
> 30 Naiḥsargika (expiation with forfeiture).
> 90 Prāyaścittīya (entailing expiation).
> 4 Prātideśanīya (which must be confessed).
> 112 Śaikṣa (rules of good conduct).
> Bhikṣunī precepts number 364 which are divided among the same categories above, in this way:
> 8 Pārājika, 27, 33, 180, 11, 112 Śaikṣa.[53]

Of these eight sorts of Prātimokṣa precepts, only the first is temporary, being observed for one day and night after which it is given up, the lay-person returning to the observance of the Five Precepts. The other seven classes are to be observed throughout life until death.

For those who wish to be established in some class of the Prātimokṣa precepts, there are a number of hindrances to their observance, so if one wishes to undertake them, one should be free of the following: 1. Having murdered one's mother or father, or an Arhat, having wounded a Buddha or having caused a schism in the Saṃgha—which five are called immediacy-karma and are a hindrance for the *arising* of restraint. 2. Again, not to gain the permission of the ruler (where required) or one's mother and father (if one wishes to go forth to the homeless life), such are hindrances to the *establishment* of restraint. 3. Then extreme youth which is described by the phrase " being unable to scare crows away " is a hindrance for the *development* of restraint. Lastly, bodily defects and peculiarities may be a hindrance to the *practice* of restraint relating to these precepts.

One should note well that birth is no hindrance, so that whether one is born into a high or low family, whether rich or poor, one may still undertake these precepts. All who are free from the above defects should observe one group of these precepts according to personal capacity and opportunity.

The way to achieve restraints not yet accomplished is twofold: by making a great effort, or with but little effort.

The following factors aid one in protecting restraint already accomplished: 1. Association with good friends (skilled teachers and virtuous companions); 2. keeping one's understanding pure and free from stain; 3. maintaining purity of precepts by knowing the stains opposing them; 4. purification born of study, and 5. bearing in mind the material causes of happiness. These five are further explained thus:

The first means that restraint can be protected by going to see well-conducted bhikṣus of good character or by listening to the discourses of such wise and learned men.[54] One who has gone forth especially, should stay near by and take instruction in Dharma from a local teacher well gifted with all the qualities of a good instructor.

Pure understanding implies that one knows which dharmas are to be abandoned and which should be developed, being diligent in learning this distinction. One should analyze one's mental-emotional continuum (which we call " mind " or citta) with the help of mindfulness and clear comprehension (smṛti-samprajanya) for this purpose. Again, recollecting one's venerable teachers one should consider how they would reprove unskillful conduct, in this way developing shame and fear of blame (hrī-apartrapā). By being well established in these virtues, one is able to protect the precepts.

The third factor, " knowing the dharmas in opposition," means that one should acquire knowledge of the causes leading to downfall of the mind's happiness. Then, having known these causes thoroughly, one should give up those leading to destruction (the mental stains) while consciously cultivating those promoting restraints. This can be done by listening to expositions of the Dharma, considering and reflecting upon it in one's mind and practicing the various teachings in the Dharma and Discipline.

Study here means that one should try to acquire training especially on the three occasions of Upa-vasatha-day (when the Prātimokṣa is chanted and Dharma-discourses are given), Varṣāvāsa (the three months Rains Residence for intensified Buddhist practice) and Pravāraṇā-day (the day ending the Rains Residence when bhikṣus invite admonition from each other and special instructions are given).

Material causes of happiness are the four requisites of life: clothing, food, shelter and medical supplies, and when the use of them gives rise to mental stains leading to downfall, one should restrain one's use of them. By the mindful and restrained use of these four requisites one can protect moral conduct.

There are four factors which lead men into unskillful action. They are:

> Ignorance,
> disrespect for the teaching,
> heedlessness, and
> the concatenation of mental defilements.

These four are called the doors to downfall and it is the duty of those who wish to protect their precepts, to renounce them. One should protect one's precepts just as one guards one's eyes. Besides this, it is necessary to develop the four skillful counterfactors of these doors to downfall:

Wisdom,
trust,
heedfulness, and
the destruction of the defilements.

(In Sanskrit: prajñā, śraddhā, appramāda, kleśakṣāya.)

It is thus easy to understand that the precepts of the Prātimokṣa restraint are similar whether followed in Theravāda or in Mahāyāna. *It is important to stress that in both branches of Buddhadharma great emphasis is placed upon the proper practice of the Prātimokṣa restraint.*

BODHISATTVA AND VAJRAYĀNA PRECEPTS

However, regarding the Bodhisattva precepts and those of Vajrayāna, these are peculiar to Mahāyāna. If one undertakes to observe the Bodhisattva Precepts of Restraint (bodhisattva-saṃvara-śīla), one has to protect oneself from the eighteen offences leading to downfall as well as from forty-six ways of misconduct. When one is established in the Vajrayāna or Adamantine Vehicle precepts, one has to guard oneself from fourteen root-causes of downfall and from eight grave evils, together with protection of the special and ordinary conduct of the Five Families (pañcagotra) as well as many other ways of conduct. As the Bodhisattva and Vajrayāna precepts are vast in number together with their divisions and methods for their practice, so they have been left unexplained in this introductory book.

Thus is finished the description of the Training in Supreme Virtue.

II. THE TRAINING IN SUPREME COLLECTEDNESS (Adhisamādhi-śikṣa)

Now, having outlined the Training in Supreme Virtue, we come to the description of the second training, that concerning collectedness (samādhi). *We have dealt with virtue first since only the person trained in virtue can train in collectedness.* Usually the mind (citta)[55] does not remain fixed for long upon one object since it is flickering here and there, being engaged with the objects of the various sense-fields, but through this training it can be made one-pointed or perfectly concentrated. When the mind is concentrated upon a skillful objcct and not disturbed, then that one-pointedness of mind is called "samādhi."

Samādhi or collectedness[56] may be analyzed into various levels of mental absorption (dhyāna). These are preceded by access collectedness (upacāra-samādhi) in which the five hindrances (nivāraṇa)[57] commonly arising in the lower planes of desire are suppressed; but when the factors of absorption (dhyānaṅga) arise, this is the level of attainment collectedness (arpaṇa-samādhi). Collectedness is of two kinds, worldly and transcendental. The worldly variety is also of two sorts: pertaining to the form realm or else to the formless realm and within these two realms there are eight levels (bhūmi), four in each realm. If by correct practice one has attained the absorptions both of form and of formlessness, then one has fulfilled the perfection of collectedness (samādhi-pāramitā).

As we pointed out above, collectedness is classified as either worldly or transcendental. Here, by " world," one should understand, are meant the three world-elements (loka-dhātu) within which all living beings are found.[58] Thus worldly collectedness is that which has worldly objects and produces a worldly result, that of calm and happiness in this life and for the next, gives rise to a celestial birth (the experience of " heaven," " paradise," etc). Unworldly or transcendental means that this sort of samādhi is aimed at freedom, its objects being essence-lessness and not-self-soulness (niḥsvabhāvatā, anātmatā). In order to achieve worldly and transcendental absorptions, one should first develop calm and insight (samatha-vipaśyanā). *Although at first one may seem to develop these aspects of samādhi separately, finally one must develop the collectedness in which they are yoked together.*[59] The aspect of collectedness which pacifies the fickleness of the mind is called " calm," while that wisdom which penetrates to the three marks (of existence)—impermanence, unsatisfactoriness, and not-self-soul—is called " insight " (vipaśyanā, literally: deep-insight).

The order of development regarding these two aspects of collectedness in the mind is first *calm* (samatha) and then *insight* (vipaśyanā), or as they may also be termed: mental development (bhāvanā), and that including thorough examination. Once the mind is well established in calm, the development including examination which yields insight becomes possible. Samatha is the calm and serene pond in which the fish (the faculty of deep insight) moves in examination. This is so because the mind at that time is fixed strongly upon its object and not easily disturbed.[60] This state is very important and the skillful karma made while dwelling in it, is very powerful and of great fruit.

There are five obstacles[61] to this development of calm which are sources of disturbance and stand opposed to tranquility. They are: 1. Mental slackness (kausīdya) creating discouragement so that the mind is not interested in the practice of collectedness. This is opposed by the mental factor called " determination " (chanda). 2. Lack of mindfulness (muśitasmṛtitā) in achieving collectedness, for if this is to be experienced there must be constant mindfulness to ensure that the mind is established with concentration upon its object. Through lack of mindfulness the object of collectedness disappears from mind. This factor, therefore, is opposed to perfect (or right) mindfulness (samyak-smṛti). 3. Next comes linking and scattering of the mind (nirmagnatā-auddhatya). " Sinking " means that the mind becomes submerged without awareness in the object, a state which bars further progress. It is necessary during meditation to be mindful of the object, while at the same time the mind should not sink into it. " Scattering " is a kind of fickleness of the mind because of which the mind cannot remain fixed upon its object. This pair of obstacles oppose clear comprehension.

4. Association with the above pair of obstacles (saṃskār-āsevanā) is itself counted as an obstacle to collectedness. In this case one knows that the mind is overpowered by sinking and scattering but still one does not make an effort to develop those factors which oppose them and are able to cure the mind. 5. It sometimes happens that having made this effort and produced the counteractive factors, one goes on practicing them at a time when they are not needed (saṃskārasevanā disassociation). This is an ignorant way of practicing and shows that the mind is not fully aware or focussed upon its object.

It is impossible to achieve the perfection of collectedness unless one puts away these five opposing factors. For training the mind to avoid these five there are eight dharmas which stand in opposition. They counteract the obstacles in this way:

1. Trust (śraddhā)	*opposes*	Mental slackness.
2. Determination (chanda)	*opposes*	
3. Perseverance (vīrya)	*opposes*	
4. Tranquility (praśrabdhi)	*opposes*	
5. Mindfulness (smṛti)	*opposes*	Lack of Mindfulness.
6. Comprehension (samprajanya)	*opposes*	Sinking and scattering.
7. Investigation (saṃskāracintanā)	*opposes*	Association with the above.
8. Equanimity (adhivāsana)	*opposes*	Non-association.

Calm should be developed by the growth of these eight qualities. Now we shall go on to discuss the nine states of mind, the six powers and the four mental activities and how, due to them, collectedness is achieved.

Nine States of Mind

1. Cittasthāpana. This is the state in which the mind first becomes unaffected by outer objects and fixed in the meditation-object.
2. Cittapravāhasaṃsthāpa is the establishment of the stream of mind, meaning that the mind is fixed upon the object for some time by compelling the mind to consider again and again the object of concentration.
3. Cittapratiharaṇa is the state when, the mind being disturbed, one "brings back" the mind to the concentration-object.
4. Cittopasthāpana in which the mind is expanded while exactly limited to the object.
5. Cittadamana—"mind-taming" which is done by seeing the ill results of distracting thoughts and defilements, also perceiving the advantages of collectedness, so that one makes efforts to put away the former while establishing the mind in the latter.
6. Cittaśamana—"mind-calming" in which feelings antagonistic to the practice of collectedness are quelled. If boredom arises regarding collectedness since the mind is still hungry for sense objects, then it is thoroughly pacified at this stage.

7. Cittavyupaśamana or the subtle pacification of mind. Even the subtle stains of mind are set aside here.
8. Cittaikoṭikaraṇa. The mind here becomes like one undisturbed stream and continues to flow along one-pointedly.
9. Samādhāna. When this state is reached, there is no need for effort since the mind is naturally one-pointed.

Six Powers

1. Śrutibala: Listening to a teacher or else reading books on the method of fixing the mind, such is meant by this first power.
2. Āśayabala: By the power of repeated thought one establishes the mind in the way of collectedness.
3. Smṛtibala: If the mind becomes distracted by some other object, it is by this power of mindfulness that it is returned to the meditation-object and established therein.
4. Samprajanyabala: By means of this power of clear comprehension one comes to know the evil results of the mental stains and the beneficial fruits derived from collectedness thus making one delight in the latter.
5. Vīryabala: This sort of skillful energy ensures that the mind is not influenced by the stains.
6. Paricāyabala: The natural and thorough acquaintance of the mind with collectedness, forced

application of mindfulness and clear comprehension being no longer needed.

Four Mental Activities

1. Manoniveśapravartak-manaskāra. By means of this activity the mind enters into the object.
2. Vicchinnapravartak-manaskāra. Although the mind may in the beginning remain in concentration for some time, every now and then distraction will arise from the obstacles of sinking, scattering and so forth. This activity returns the mind to its object.
3. Avicchinnapravartak-manaskāra. Through this activity the mind is established in the object for a long period thus giving no chance to distractions.
4. Āyatanapravartak-manaskāra. When all the hindrances to collectedness have been set aside, it is through this activity that the mind is held effortlessly upon its object.

The Successive Attainment of Collectedness [62]

Now having given an outline of the various factors involved in the approach to collectedness, the subject to be explained here will be the progress through the nine states of mind and the hindrances which are encountered in them and how the various powers and mental activities bring them to an end.

As I said above, *the first power* consists of listening to the teaching and making the mind learn about the objects of concentration. Those who have heard this kind of teaching and who desire to experience collectedness, do not allow their minds to stray upon exterior objects. When the mind begins to be established in this object, it is called *the first state of mind.* Although the mind begins to be established in the object, it fails to be concentrated upon the same object for a long time. Thoughts pour from the mind like water in a waterfall and it seems as though a veritable flood of thoughts arise. The truth is that the mind has always been in this state but never before was one aware of it, since one had never turned one's gaze within before. Now that the mind is turned inward because of the practice of mindfulness and clear comprehension, these thoughts become known. Just as upon a great and crowded highway, a careless person may not be aware how crowded it really is unless he examines carefully to see the different sorts and numbers of people, so in the same way the mind begins to know the variety and range of thoughts comprising it. This should not be regarded as a fault of practice but quite a natural experience for one beginning to take up concentration.

While experiencing the first state of mind, it is by means of *the second power* that the mind is repeatedly established upon the object. In this way the mind becomes restrained for some time by this power and so reaches *the second state of mind.* Here thoughts sometimes arise and disturb the mind after which they die away and it is then that the meditator realizes for the first time the stopping of thoughts. Two faults are commonly found here: sinking and scattering. If the former then the mind sinks gently into the object and a sort of sleep is the result, while the latter makes the mind fickle and run after other objects. The result of these is that one's collectedness loses power and force. When this occurs, one should fix the mind unwaveringly upon the object and where this occurs, it is known as *the first mental activity*.

However, if after the mind has been earnestly tied to the object, it is continually being disturbed by other objects, then it must be established again upon the object of concentration by *the third power* (of mindfulness). One will then reach *the third state of mind.*

As I said above, whenever the mind is not energetic and hence gets discouraged due to the faults of sinking and so on, then it is directed by the third power to return to the concentration-object. Likewise, this power of mindfulness is needed to limit the mind when expanded, from straying to other objects. This is *the fourth state of mind.*

While practicing concentration, thoughts and stains appear repeatedly and this is because the meditator does not know the unskillful and distracting results to be expected from them, nor does he realize the skilled fruits of collectedness. When by way of the fourth power (clear comprehension) one notices and comes to know these faults, then they can be properly dealt with by means of this power. This means that stains already arisen are cut off, the mind being well established in the object, and when this occurs it is known as the *fifth state of mind.*

From time to time the mind is liable to become dissatisfied with concentration so that from the arising of boredom there is the experience of scattering. By means of the power of clear comprehension the bad fruits of this scatteredness are known thereby not permitting the mind to entertain boredom. This is called *the sixth state of mind.*

As far as this stage of practice is concerned, although faults and stains have been suppressed by reflection upon their unsatisfactory results for the future, this does not mean that they will not arise again. For this reason the meditator should always beware. Whenever these stains become manifest in the mind, then the real value of awareness may be seen for whatever the stain, whether greed, lust, singing, and so forth, and whether arising in a gross or in a subtle form, it can be ended with this awareness where it is supported by earnestness and effort. This is *the seventh state of mind.*

Although from the third up to the seventh state the mind has been concentrated to a greater or lesser extent, even when well established in the object, stains such as sinking and scattering and so on will cause distraction from time to time though perhaps only after long intervals. This results in one's collectedness being broken and at such a time this is restored by *the second mental activity.* This activity has its application in all states of mind from the third to the seventh.

Monks at prayer – Thekchen Choling, Dharmsala, India

Art work – monks at Dalhousie, India

If the meditator develops both the third and fourth powers to counteract scattering and *the fifth power* against sinking, then these two stains will not arise as hindrances to collectedness. As a result of this one's practice proceeds like an unbroken stream, this being *the eighth state of mind.*

While experiencing this state if one makes an effort carefully and persistently, then these two stains have no power to break into collectedness so that it proceeds unbroken and quite undisturbed, *the third mental activity* thus being found in this state.

Persistently and continuously developing collectedness, it is through *the sixth power* that the object becomes very clear. In this state, the mind is effortlessly concentrated on the object without the support either of mindfulness or of clear comprehension. One has then reached *the ninth state of mind.* Just as a man who has learnt the scriptures well, may while chanting them, let his mind wander elsewhere, yet there is no hindrance to his chanting, so the mind which has been previously well established in the object, is now fixed there effortlessly and without any hindrance. The current of collectedness is now able to flow for a long time without effort made by the practicer, this being the *fourth mental activity.* The ninth state of mind is also called "access collectedness" (upacāra samādhi).

DIAGRAMMATIC SUMMARY OF PROGRESS THROUGH THE NINE STATES

1st Power	——→	1st State		
		↓		
2nd Power	——→	2nd State	←—→	1st Mental Activity
		↓		
3rd Power	——→	3rd State	←—→	2nd Mental Activity
		↓		
3rd Power	——→	4th State	←—→	2nd Mental Activity
		↓		
4th Power	——→	5th State	←—→	2nd Mental Activity
		↓		
4th Power	——→	6th State	←—→	2nd Mental Activity
		↓		
5th Power	——→	7th State	←—→	2nd Mental Activity
		↓		
3rd, 4th, 5th Powers	→	8th State	←—→	3rd Mental Activity
		↓		
6th Power	——→	9th State	←—→	4th Mental Activity

Calm is found even in the mind of a meditator who begins to practice for the attainment of collectedness. As the strength of calm increases so stiffness both of mind and body decrease. This stiffness, dullness or unworkability of mind is associated with heaviness and mental inactivity, all of which are aspects of that root-cause of the mental stains, delusion (moha). When we say that calm stands opposed to stiffness, we mean that this calm or samatha is accompanied by lightness both of mind and body.[63] In a calm mind, joy (prīti) arises and because of this the mind becomes established in the meditation object. The calm of mind also gives rise to a tranquil and relaxed body, such bodily peace being very helpful to the meditator.

As one progresses with collectedness this joy tends to decrease while equanimity (upekṣā) replaces it, the mind thereby being established in the object with greater stability, an experience known as samādhi-upacāra-acala-praśrabdhi (lit: the unshaken tranquility of access to collectedness) and with it one enters a state very close to the first absorption (dhyāna).

By continuing one's practice in this way, one does in fact reach the first absorption. We have already said that there are three great levels (bhūmi), sometimes called world-elements (dhātu) but these may be further subdivided to make up a total of nine levels:

1.	sensuous-existence level	(kāma-bhūmi)
2.	first absorption level	(prathama-dhyāna-bhūmi)
3.	second absorption level	(dvitīya-dhyāna-bhūmi)
4.	third absorption level	(tritīya-dhyāna-bhūmi)
5.	fourth absorption level	(caturtha-dhyāna-bhūmi)
6.	sphere of infinite space level	(ākāśānantyāyatana-bhūmi)
7.	sphere of infinite consciousness level	(vijñānānantyāyatana-bhūmi)
8.	sphere of no-thingness level	(ākiñcanyāyatana-bhūmi)

9. sphere of neither-perception-nor-nonperception-level (naiva-samjñā-nāsaṃjñāyatana-bhūmi) also called the summit of becoming (bhavāgra).

These successive levels are attained by having no attachment for them and by seeing the advantages of the levels higher than those already attained together with the disadvantages of those already reached.

These absorption-attainments (dhyāna-samāpatti), that is the last eight of these nine levels, are causal factors since by means of their attainment (when a man) one may be reborn among the celestials of form or formlessness (according to the type of absorption reached).

The Method for the Attainment of the Absorptions

As I remarked above, the worldly attainment of the absorptions is of two sorts, of form and of formlessness, both of which have four levels.

Each of these absorptions has two stages: of approach and of accomplishment. So now I shall point out the method for their attainment.

First Absorption. In the approach stage to the first absorption, there are these six mental activities:

1. " experiencing characteristics " (lakṣaṇapratisaṃvedi-manaskāra).
2. " leading to Freedom " (ādhimokṣīka-manaskāra).
3. " near to isolation "—from desire (prāviveja-manaskāra).
4. " increaser of joy " (ratisaṃgrāhaka-manaskāra).
5. " the examiner " (mimāṃsaka-manaskāra).
6. " accomplished in applying " (prayogajñiṣṭha-manaskāra).

Now, what application do these activities have? The first is when, by means of the two sorts of wisdom —of hearing (learning) and of thinking (reflection)— one sees the disadvantages of the approaches to absorption in the desire level (kāma-bhūmi) and the advantages of the first absorption. This activity of experiencing these characteristics is rough by way of thought-conception (vitarka) and subtle through thought-examination (vicāra).

When the first activity is transformed by practice into development-wisdom (bhāvanā-maya-prajña which is insight or vipaśyanā of the lower levels), it is known as the second mental activity "leading to freedom."

One should note that in the mental continuum of beings there are both gross and subtle taints (mala). Only the gross taints among these are destroyed by the absorptions while the subtle ones can only be destroyed by the full development-wisdom acquired at the time of knowing the Noble Paths[64] which pertain to the supermundane (lokottara); while the nine levels given above are all mundane (wordly in the sense of being within the wheel of birth-death). Through the attainment only of the latter, the gross taints of the level below are destroyed (thus permitting the meditator to advance). Now, in the approaching state of the first absorption, the gross stains of the desire-level are destroyed. When through the power of development-wisdom one succeeds in destroying the gross stains of the desire-level,[65] this is called the third mental activity " near to isolation " from desire.

When by practicing this mental activity, one succeeds in destroying the middling stains attached to the desire-level, this is called the fourth mental activity known as " increaser of joy."

At the time when both strong and medium stains have been destroyed, then it is necessary to bring to mind the subtle stains because compared with the others, they are very difficult to perceive. For this reason the fifth mental activity is essential as an "examiner" which sees whether these subtle stains are present or not.

Having come to see the subtle stains by way of the fifth, one knows that the mental continuum is still stained by them, so one feels the need to destroy them. The mental activity opposing these subtle stains is the sixth one called "accomplished in application."

As a result of the accomplishment of these mental activities, there is the experience of the fruit of that accomplishment—the first absorption. It is a characteristic of all these mental activities to see the grossness of the stage below with all its faults, while viewing the stage above as faultless and calm. This method of consideration helps one both along the mundane and along the supermundane (or transcendental) paths.

There are five factors composing the first absorption: thought-conception, thought-examination, joy, bliss and one-pointedness (vitarka, vicāra, prīti, sukha, ekāgratā). Of these five, the first two are those opposing the mental stains, joy and bliss are the results of practice, while one-pointedness of mind is called the basis for the other four. If both thought-conception and thought-examination are found in the first absorption, then it is just known as "accomplished," but if the first of these is absent then it is called "specially accomplished."[66]

Second Absorption. In the approach states to each absorption, all the six mental activities are found. In this case, by way of them one perceives the faults of the first absorption as well as the peace of the state above it. The accomplished stage of the second absorption has four factors: inner purity, joy resulting from collectedness, bliss and one-pointedness. Among these four, the first opposes mental stains, while joy and bliss are the result of practice, the last one being the basis of the other three. "Inner purity" is the collective name given to mindfulness, tranquility and equanimity, because of its destruction of the mental stains.[67]

Third Absorption. As before, the six mental activities are found in its approach stage where they make it possible to see the faults of the second absorption and the advantages of developing further (toward the accomplishment of the third). By being detached from the second, one attains the accomplished state of the third which has five factors: mindfulness, clear comprehension, equanimity, bliss devoid of joy and one-pointedness. Of these five, the first three oppose mental stains, while the fourth is a resultant and the fifth as before, the basis.[68]

Fourth Absorption. The approach state with the six mental activities is the same as above. Seeing the disadvantages of the third absorption and the benefit of the fourth, by detachment from the former state and striving for the latter, one comes to realize its accomplishment. There are four factors in its composition: mindful purity, equanimous purity, equanimous feeling and one-pointedness. Here the first two are opposed to the stains, the third is the result of practice, while the fourth is the basis.[69]

The mindfulness found in the fourth absorption is specially distinguished by calling it " purified " because it is free from the eight faults found in absorptions. These are: thought-conception, thought-examination, bliss, unsatisfactoriness, mental pleasure, mental pain, inhalation and exhalation. They may indeed be called thorns for the attainment of collectedness. Of these, the first two are faults of the first absorption and are compared to flames. Sensual happiness arising from the five bases is a fault of the second absorption. Mental pleasure and pain which arise through the sixth base (mind) are faults in the third absorption, while the fourth when perfectly accomplished, is free from all these eight faults.

The Fruits of Accomplished Absorptions

Depending on the development of accomplished absorptions, each one may be termed weak, medium or strong, birth taking place accordingly, the three strengths of each absorption corresponding to three sub-levels within each plane of the level of form.[70]

The subtle imperceptible-form (avijñapti-rūpa, see section on the five heaps) which is accumulated by the practice of the absorptions, is called the ripened fruit (vipāka-phala) of the respective stage reached.

When a concentrated mind is the goal achieved, this is the natural result, a fruit which "flows out of" one's practice (nisyanda-phala). Material things, requisites or comforts gained as a result of practice (from the esteem of others) are the fruits called "extra-obtained" (adhipati-phala).

Four Formless Accomplishments (arūpi-samāpatti)

After having attained the fourth absorption, one turns away completely from touch, sight and physical dharmas, even subtle ones, while developing the thought: "All dharmas are like infinite space." One should fix the mind on this and develop it. Upon development, one has achieved the Sphere of Infinite Space. Having accomplished this one should go on to develop the thought: "Consciousness is like the infinity of space." After some time one will achieve the Sphere of Infinite Consciousness. These two accomplishments having been won, and perceiving that they have objects and are established upon objects, one should develop the thought: "No thing is to be grasped," thus coming to accomplish the Sphere of No-thingness. Finally, having come to see that these three spheres have objects even though they are subtle, one should develop further by thinking thus: "While there is no gross perception there is no absence of subtle perception" in this way, accomplishing the sphere of neither-perception-nor-non-perception. This last accomplishment is called the Summit of Becoming.

Throughout this formless element, the form-heap is completely extinct and only the four mental heaps (nāma-skandha) are found. Although the sub-levels found in the form-element are not present in the formless realms, even here beings are born long or short-lived and of greater or lesser brilliance according to the power of collectedness developed. After being born into this formless realm, if one continues diligently to practice collectedness (for the attainment of those spheres not yet attained) and if one thereby expands the power of one's collectedness, this may result in the special fruits of being established in extremely long life in the formless realm.

Special Virtues and Knowledges

The attainment of the absorptions generally is difficult but they are of great importance, for by their accomplishment one becomes endowed with special virtues and knowledges. Both Buddhists and outsiders can gain these but whereas outsiders may regard them as an end in themselves (as divine blessings, union with God, miracles, etc.) for Buddhists they are only a means to attain the " Paths " and " Fruits " which will be explained later and which are experienced after the exercise of wisdom (prajñā). As these various attainments are forerunners of the " Paths" and " Fruits," so those within the Conqueror's teaching should be educated in their practice and attainment.

By the practice of the four accomplished states of the form-absorptions (rūpa-dhyāna), one attains to the four unlimiteds (apramāṇa) and the five superknowledges (abhijñā). Firstly, the four unlimiteds are friendliness, compassion, joy-with-others, and equanimity (maitrī, karuṇā, muditā, upekṣā). They are called " limitless " because the mental object of them is " all beings." Friendliness means that one develops amity toward all beings and this counteracts feelings of hatred. Compassion is developed when seeing the sufferings of others so that one wishes to share their troubles and to help them, this being opposed to the attitude of callous indifference. Joy-with-others is the feeling of happiness experienced when one sees the happiness of others whether it pertains to material gains or to mental states, and thus one overcomes envy. Equanimity is necessary in those situations where one cannot bring about any change and in which, therefore, one should remain aloof. Its development leads to detachment both from delight at an enemy fallen upon affliction and from sorrow when one's friends and relatives suffer.

The superknowledges (abhijñā) are various worldly powers which arise in one who has practiced the four form-absorptions. These knowledges are five, as follows:

1. divyacakṣu, the divine-eye by which one is able to see forms, even subtle ones, both far and near.
2. divyaśrota, the divine-ear whereby sounds though very faint can be heard from far away.
3. paracittajñāna, knowledge of others' minds, possessing which one is able to know what is passing in the minds of others.

4. pūrvanivāsānusmṛti, " past-dwellings-recollection, " that is, the knowing of past lives both of one's own continuity and in the continuities of others, remembering such details as place of birth, name and status of one's family and many other matters.
5. cyutyupapattijñāna, knowledge of the death-moment and the rebirth-moment of beings who arise in their several bourns according to their karma.

These knowledges are peculiar to the realm of form and cannot arise in the formless realm. The latter has, however, its own peculiarities including the accomplishment of non-perception (asaṃjñā-samāpatti) and the experience of cessation (nirodha-samāpatti). The first is based upon the attainment of the fourth absorption and is a state in which all gross forms of perception cease to exist Then, with the Summit of Becoming as base one may enter the accomplishment of cessation when the stream of mind and mental dharmas (citta, caitta-dharma) can be stopped completely for a predetermined time.

It is the duty of those who earnestly practice the teachings of the Three Vehicles that they should accomplish the states of collectedness and so become endowed with their virtues, and practicing further, develop the unlimiteds, superknowledges and the accomplishments.

Thus is finished the description of the Training in Supreme Collectedness.

III. THE TRAINING IN SUPREME WISDOM (Adhiprajñāśikṣā)

This is the last of the three trainings. Wisdom (prajñā) means that special kind of knowledge whereby one examines skillful and unskillful karma. It increases through the practice of mind-development (bhāvanā). After completion it is known as the Perfection of Wisdom. Here we may distinguish three sorts of wisdom:

1. paramarthaparicchedaka-prajñā (wisdom analyzing the supermundane or Absolute). By means of this sort of wisdom one has knowledge, at first indirectly, of not-self-soul (anātman) but when this wisdom is complete then one understands anātman from direct personal experience.
2. samvṛttaparicchedaka-prajñā (wisdom analyzing the relative). By way of this wisdom the five branches of knowledge are explained. These are: śabda-vidyā, the study of language; hetu-vidyā, the study of logic; adhyātmika-vidyā, the study of religion; cikitsā-vidyā, the study of medicine; and śilpa-vidyā the study of arts and crafts.
3. sattvarthaparicchedaka-prajñā (wisdom analyzing the advantages of beings). Through this one accomplishes the advantage of all beings, both of this world and of other realms. This kind of wisdom cognizes the dharmas which are " beautiful-to-do " (kalyāṇakāraka) and accomplishes them in a befitting manner.

Of these three sorts of wisdom, the first is supreme. Hence, one ought to make special efforts for its perfection. The teaching of not-self-soul (anātman) is actually found everywhere in Buddhist thought and practice and for its explanation there are numbers of methods but these all alike lead to the Perfection of Wisdom. This supreme wisdom is that which knows "no self-nature" (nihsvabhāvata) as the Absolute Truth. The teachers of the Mādhyamika Prasaṅgika school have made great efforts to explain clearly this teaching of not-self-soul. The following discussion will therefore be along the lines of those teachers.

As I may as well emphasize again, the teaching of no-self-soul is upheld by all schools of Buddhist thought since all alike recognize the ātman-view, that is adhering to belief in some permanent soul-entity, as the root of all trouble. To suppose that things exist independently, have a "self-nature," is the ātman-view and this in turn is ignorance. It is thus because of this ātman-view that beings are wandering on in the realms of birth and death. The ātman-view is then the root of saṃsāra or the wandering-on. However, for one who is freed, such as an Arhat, this ātman-view is destroyed (since he has penetrated to the truth of no-ātman). It is only possible to eradicate this root of ignorance by the insight (vipaśyanā) called not-ātman-knowledge (nairātmya-jñāna) *and by this alone*. It is therefore essential that one develops the highest aspect of insight so as to see no-ātman personally.

No-ātman (or not-soul-self) has two aspects: the no-ātman of the person (pudgala-nairātmya) and the no-ātman of mental events (dharma-nairātmya). Both are explained by using the term "no-self-nature" (nihsvabhāva), that is that both persons and the events into which they may be analyzed are, all alike, without self-nature or substance. Now, if first we understand well the no-ātman of persons, it will be easier to comprehend the no-ātman of events.

To establish a rational understanding of the no-ātman of the person there are many methods of explanation, the most important being called "the sundering of the views of oneness and not-oneness" (ekāneka-viyuktatva). This will be explained below under four headings, their Sanskrit names being: 1. niṣcdhya-viniścaya-marma; 2. vyāpti-viniścaya-marma; 3. ekatva-viyukta-viniścaya-marma; 4. anekatva-viyukta-viniścay-marma.

The first is explained as follows. The object to be negated is the self or soul-concept. But it is impossible to negate this unless first we have knowledge of how the ātman-view conceives of a self-soul. Here one should say that the ātman is to be negated both in its subtle and in its gross forms. If only the gross form of ātman-conception is negated, then the subtle aspect remains intact. Now, the ātman-view whereby one conceives of an independent and self-existent entity called "ātman" or self-soul, veers toward eternalism which means that one falls into an extreme view, that of eternalism-belief (śāśvata-dṛṣṭi). On the other hand one has also to be careful, for if all the sense-objects perceived by the six sense bases are negated, then one annihilates relative or conventional truth (that there is a living person who goes on from day to day, etc.). If one follows this course consistently then one will be liable to hold to the other extreme view of annihilationism (utcheda-dṛṣṭi).

Here one should avoid both the above extremes and to do this one has to examine the ātman-view which is the conception of an independent entity. This ātman-view is of two kinds, namely conceptualized (parikalpita) and innate (sahaja). The grasping of an ātman based on the various sorts of philosophical systems contrived by the soul-believers is called the conceptualized ātman-view. This kind of ātman-view is limited to those beings who believe in those particular systems of thought and hence is not found in all beings. However, the grasping or acceptance of an "I am" in the natural way without recourse to philosophical concepts is called the innate ātman-view and is found in all beings. If we examine it closely, we will find that this kind of ātman-view grasps the "I" as an independent entity as though it stands independent of the five heaps. *If examined, all such views will be found to be based upon the five heaps or upon one of them. Hence, grasping at an ātman is done in terms of one of these five.*[71] To understand this clearly is called "recognition of objects to be negated" (niṣedhya-viniścaya-marma).

The second point to view here is the existence of the ātman when taken to be independent. Then the question will arise whether it is apart from the five heaps or not apart (non-different) from them. But there is nothing apart from them. So this question is irrelevant.[72] Then " I-ness " neither can be apart from the five heaps nor not apart from them. The understanding of this point is called " recognition of the uniform " (vyāpti-viniścaya-marma).

Thirdly, one should consider that if the self-soul (ātman) and the five heaps are of the same nature, (regardless of the fact that they seem different to the undeveloped mind), then they will be one and the same. Why is this? Because if they were really of the same nature, then this supposed real nature (of non-difference) and this seeming nature (perceived by the undeveloped mind) could only appear different in the realm of relative truth and could not be any different at all in Absolute Truth. This means that where sameness of the same nature is assumed, there can be no difference between relative and Absolute Truth. It is for this reason that we have said that if ātman and the five heaps are of the same nature, then they will not be different.

If we then accept these two truths as not-different, various fallacies will be committed: (1) if not-different, then in a being there would be as many selves as there are heaps. (A human being possessing all five heaps would then possess five ātman.) (2) Again, if a man had only one ātman, there could be only one heap. (3) Or again, as the heaps have all the same nature to arise and pass away, then the ātman (or soul-self) would also arise and pass away. So by various dialectical tests, it becomes clear that the ātman and the five heaps cannot be the same self-existent unit. This is to have thorough knowledge of the weak spot sundering (the view of) oneness (of ātman and the five heaps) or in Sanskrit: ekatva-viyukta-viniścaya-marma.

Then fourth, as we have negated the sameness of an ātman with the heaps, we should now, through dialectic, negate their total exclusiveness. If the ātman is totally different from the heaps then a close examination should reveal this. But then if they are different from the point of view of relative truth (as the undeveloped mind assumes), then they cannot be different in Absolute Truth (since Absolute Truth is always a truth differing from the relative truth). But this would be in contradiction to the claim that they are totally different.

In this proposition, we should have to accept that ātman and the heaps were quite unrelated, being totally different things. Such being the case we shall have to accept that ātman will be free from the characteristics of the heaps in terms of arising, existence and disappearance. Thus, one who believes in this kind of ātman-view, that ātman is totally different from the elements of personality, will have to be able to show that ātman existing independently of and having no relation to the five heaps—and this is impossible to do[73] (since all the possible means of cognizing an ātman, soul, self, etc. lie within the five heaps). Therefore, it can never be correct to hold the view that the ātman and the heaps are totally different. This is called thorough knowledge of the weak spot sundering (the view of) not-oneness (of the ātman and the five heaps) or in Sanskrit: anekatva-viyukta-viniścaya-marma.

For achieving an understanding of no-self-nature (in the person) one should know in this way the reasons why the ātman and the heaps are neither the same nor different.

One may arrive at understanding of no-self-nature in another way through the dialectic method called anupalabdhi (the unobtainability of the conditions necessary to prove the object). The no-self-nature of the ātman can be explained by the following analogy: A man has only two possible places to look for a cow thought to be missing, but upon making a thorough search in both spots, he fails to find her. He knows that the cow cannot possibly be elsewhere, it being useless to consider a third place, so the fruitlessness of his search becomes apparent and with it his mistaken assumption (of a lost cow) is revealed. Likewise, the assumed independent existence of the ātman after one has searched for it both within and without the five heaps, must be seen to be non-existent. *Belief in an independent ātman (soul) is actually the result of mental activity.* Such ideas of an ātman are proved an illusion and proved logically invalid by the sundering (of the views) of oneness and not-oneness so that one arrives at ātma-śunyatā (voidness of the ātman) which is synonymous with no-ātman of the person (pudgala-nairātmya). In this way and by the force of this dialectic there arises in one who practices thus right view of the Middle Practice-Path.

As we have dealt briefly with the no-ātman of the person, we will now explain the no-ātman of mental events (dharma-nairātmya). Generally, things such as a pot are regarded as though they existed independently. In reality, a pot is a result of the combination of a number of causes such as clay, the potter, his effort, heat and so forth. That means that its existence is dependent upon many other factors different from the finished product called 'pot' so that one may easily see that it has no independent existence. If it was really independent then it must have been self-originated (svāyambhu) but upon examination, we do not find anything of this nature. Now, all experienceable dharmas which make up the world we are aware of, are of a like nature to the pot, requiring supporting conditions for their arising and existence. This aspect of existence is the most important proof that the nature of the dharmas is also one of no-self-nature. This is in fact Absolute Truth. Although we may feel that dharmas (mental events) have a being or nature in themselves, Absolute Truth reveals them to be void of such a nature. Believing that the truth of things lies in the way in which we perceive them (as self-existing entities) is called the view of the self-hood of dharmas (dharmātma-dṛṣṭi), this being equivalent to assuming sense data to be ultimately true. But in order to know the truth which is hidden (by our own mental stains such as avidyā, ignorance,) the dharmas should be examined in the light of the four dialectical approaches given above. Examining them in this way one gets rid of the self-imposed view that dharmas have being in themselves, coming thus to penetrate to the ultimate voidness. By penetrating to this one will ascertain that the whole world is just conceptualization, and its existence relative. This is the knowledge whereby one realizes the no-ātman of dharmas.

When one arrives at the right understanding of no-self-nature of both persons and of dharmas, then the world as a whole is comprehended in terms of cause and effect, subject and object, its very existence being dependent on a multitude of causes. In fact, the processes affecting both living and non-living things, can best be understood by establishing the truth of no-ātman of dharmas. One may do so by ascertaining the views which other people hold regarding conditioned dharmas so that one comes to understand Dependent Arising in terms of the void.[74] *When one perceives Dependent Arising as the void and the void as Dependent Arising, then with insight one perceives the essence of all Lord Buddha's discourses.*

But for the comprehension of the void (even in an intellectual way), the dialectic of sundering the views of oneness and not-oneness, is not regarded as sufficient and there are other dialectical methods to reinforce knowledge of the truth. Among them are:

(1) Vajra-kaṇa-yukti, the vajra-particle method involving a thorough examination of the four

condemnable ways to show that:

all dharmas are not born——{ from themselves, from other causes, from both, from neither (causelessly).

(2) Sad-asad-anupapatti-yukti, the arising of truth and non-truth method consisting of examination to refute tendencies of:

1. similarizing the nature of cause and effect,
2. arising out of a self-existing other cause,
3. arising out of both the original and supporting causes,
4. causelessness.

(3) catuṣkoṭyutpādānupatti-yukti, the four-cornered (logic showing that) production is unproduced. This proceeds by an examination of the production of all dharmas, condemning thereby that:

1. One cause produces many effects,
2. Many causes produce one effect,
3. Many causes produce many effects, and
4. One cause produces an effect.

(4) Pratītya-samutpannatva-yukti, the method of Dependent Arising which proceeds by an examination of all dharmas to show that they arise dependently and are thus insubstantial and void of an ātman.

From the exercise of this dialectic there arises knowledge of the deep meaning of voidness or no-ātman-ness and when this understanding is obtained, it should be developed and realized by means of collectedness which may be with or without thought-conception (savitarka, avitarka) for this is the manner in which the Training in Supreme Wisdom is applied.

Thus is finished the description of the Training in Supreme Wisdom.

THE PATH

(*mārga*)

THE highest of these supreme trainings is that of wisdom and something of its nature has been explained in the previous section. Now we shall show in brief the way to practice this wisdom-training together with virtue and collectedness. There are different applications of this threefold training according to the aspiration followed, the path practiced and the end result desired. Hence, we shall describe the path of one who is a disciple (śrāvaka, lit: "hearkener") and who aspires to be an Arhat ("one who is worthy" because of the destruction of the stains); the path of one who wishes to become a Silent Buddha (pratyeka-buddha, lit: "a Buddha for himself"), and finally that of the Bodhisattva (a being who vows to attain enlightenment for the good of all sentient beings) who treads the path leading to the attainment of perfect Buddhahood (samyak-sambuddhatva).

THE DISCIPLES' VEHICLE (OR PATH)
(Śravakayāna)

This path has different stages beginning with: Sambhāramārga (The Path of Accumulation). It is well known that beings enmeshed in the net of karma and mental stains are wandering here and there within the wheel of birth and death, existing temporarily in many realms of birth from the highest, Bhavāgra or the summit of existence, down to the lowest, Avīci, the hell "without respite."[75] The whole wheel revolved by causes (such as ignorance and craving) and by effects (such as the various forms of unsatisfactory experience, disease, aging, death and birth) is verily duhkha itself and everywhere defiled by the presence of mental stains and deficiencies. One should regard it as a stream of the heaps of grasping (the five impermanent heaps comprising one's personality which are grasped at trying to make them "one's own," upadāna-skandha). The duhkha experienced by beings because of their grasping is various but may be divided into:

1. duhkha-duhkhatā (suffering of unsatisfactoriness)
2. viparināma-duhkhatā (suffering of deterioration)
3. saṃskāra-duhkhatā (suffering of conformations)

The first means bodily and mental pain which is actually felt and which cannot be other than unsatisfactory. The second is the oppressive nature of all conditioned things which are bound to change and deteriorate, while the third means the unsatisfactory nature of all that is formed or conditioned because of the dependent and precarious mode of its existence.

It should be the aim of him who practices Dharma to have a clear understanding of these various categories of duhkha and to perceive how they affect him personally [76] so that non-attachment arises regarding the world together with a strong desire to gain freedom from worldliness. When one feels the arising of this desire and so gains incentive to attain the goal this is to enter upon the Path of Accumulation. In this way one departs from what is not the path and enters upon the path leading to freedom. In the course of one's practice, one accumulates all the necessary merits [77] for the great journey about to be undertaken.

This first path is threefold, being weak, medium or strong according to one's practice of such contemplations as the unbeautiful (aśubha-bhāvanā designed to remedy for instance, the attraction of a beautiful girl, for if one were to consider that which is called "beautiful" as just a conglomeration of bones, blood and other revolting things, then the lustful or greedy mind would be cured), mindfulness of breathing (to cure the distracted mind), and other aspects of mindfulness (for awareness of the Dharma in one's daily life). Through the practice of these, the wrong views increasing the stains called inversions (viparyāsa) are gradually weakened but not yet destroyed. The inversions consist of (perceptual, mental and philosophical) views which regard the unbeautiful as beautiful, the unsatisfactory as happiness, the impermanent as permanent, and the state of no-ātman as being endowed with a soul. Since these inversions are weakened, the mind of one thus practicing does not tend to the accumulation of worldly wealth nor to its enjoyment, but loses interest in such worldliness. On the contrary, his mind advances toward purification and the necessary destruction of the stains which must precede freedom. From his practice he gains one or some of the five superknowledges and is possessed of the power to project himself in different forms.

Prayogamārga, The Path of Endeavor, is the second of these stages. Being endowed with the virtues of the Path of Accumulation, one advances on the way leading to freedom. Henceforth, one who is on this path has ever-increasing virtues and he becomes endowed with new virtues not possessed by him previously. In this second path he advances through the four stages called "aids to penetration,"[78] (nirvedha-bhāgiyā) which are heat, summits, patience, and sublime dharma.

In these four stages there arises development-wisdom (which can also be called vipaśyanā, or insight) penetrating to the general marks of the Four Noble Truths, this wisdom becoming sharper as one progresses from stage to stage. Because of this, the three marks (of existence): impermanence, unsatisfactoriness and no-ātman become progressively clear. The five skillful faculties also (kuśalendriya) [79] and the five powers become manifest in one so that one attains many virtues. Of the four stages mentioned above, the first called " supreme dharma " is the final state of the unenlightened worldling. After its experience, one fares upon the transcendental paths, having joined the family of the noble ones (Ārya).

The third path is called the Path of Insight, or Darśanamārga and is concerned with seeing by transcendental insight the Four Noble Truths in sixteen different aspects.[80] In this stage one has direct vision of no-self-nature in the Four Noble Truths so that by this Path of Insight one rightly destroys all the stains which are to be destroyed in this path, whether they relate to the world-elements of sensual pleasure, form, or formlessness. These stains are of three sorts grouped under: the view that the body is owned by oneself (satkāyadṛṣṭi), scepticism (vicikitsa) and attachment to vows and rites, (śīlavrata-paramarśa). From their destruction arise the special virtues of the noble one and from the moment of these virtues' arising, one is counted a member of the Jewel of the Saṃgha (saṃgharatna). The stains which are destroyed on the Path of Insight are adventitious stains (āgantuka-kleśa) while the innate stains (sahaja-kleśa) have not yet gone to destruction. For this reason, after having attained the Path of Insight, one takes up the practice of the whole Noble Eightfold Path, together with the mind development of voidness.

The Noble Eightfold Path [81]

(ārya-aṣṭaṅgika-mārga)

The eight factors of this path are as follows:

(1) samyak-dṛṣṭi, perfect understanding, in which two stages in the Aryan Path are distinguished: samāhita-mārga, when in a state of collectedness one sees the Four Noble Truths face to face, afterwards bringing back this experience to practice it in daily life (pṛsthạ-labdha-mārga).

(2) samyak-saṃkalpa, perfect examination whereby the causes for the realization of voidness and its characteristics are examined. This voidness is the essence of all Lord Buddha's discourses, while this examination ascertains the ways and means by which others may be led to understand.

(3) samyak-vāk, perfect speech. Although the void is not manifold (niṣprapañca) and thus cannot be expressed in words, still one can talk about it from a practical point of view. It is this perfect speech which causes others to know about the unmanifold void by teaching them in speech and by the written word, so that they become established in perfect understanding. It is thus the freedom from all false speech.[82]

(4) samyak-karmanta, perfect action. Naturally, the conduct of the noble ones always accords

with the Dharma so that this factor establishes the practicer in pure precepts. It may also be called "pure bodily action."

(5) samyak-ājīva, perfect livelihood. Āryas or noble ones always have pure livelihood since their living is never mixed up with wrong ways of life. The noble one's conduct is free of crooked bodily and verbal expression, such as exhibiting his virtues in front of others.

(6) samyak-vyāyāma, perfect effort which is a kind of mind-development with use of the "thinking wisdom" to develop the experience of voidness already realized.

(7) samyak-smṛti, perfect mindfulness. When Āryas attain calm and insight their main objects for reflection and investigation are the Four Noble Truths. The function of perfect mindfulness is to maintain these objects in their minds, not letting these truths become lost. The stain which causes forgetfulness (or muṣitasmṛti), is opposed by this path-factor.

(8) samyak-samādhi, perfect collectedness. This pure collected state of mind stands opposed to and frees one from the stains of sinking and scattering. By this perfect collectedness, one advances further and further along the path.

This Noble Eightfold Path can be divided[83] into four divisions: cutting off, cognizing, arousing trust and opposing (avacchedaka, avabodhaka, viśvāsadhāyaka, and pratipakṣa). In this way, perfect understanding *cuts off* wrong views (mithyā-dṛṣṭi) and penetrates to the void, this being of the first division. Perfect examination helps others to *cognize* the true nature of reality. Perfect speech, action and livelihood *arouse trust* so that others too practice them. The last three factors of the path, perfect effort, mindfulness and collectedness, are *opposed* to the mental stains.

Bhāvanāmārga is the Path of Development. By persistent practice of the Noble Eightfold Path, one enters the Path of Development where the stains to be destroyed by mind-development are in fact destroyed. In the process of discarding them there are two methods: the "gradual" and the "single-stroke." In the former, one gradually destroys gross, medium and subtle stains attached first to the realm of sensual pleasures and then those concerning each one of the absorptions of form and finally those found in the formless attainments, ending with the Summit of Existence. By the latter method, one practicing this path destroys first of all the strong stains of all realms, then the medium ones, finally destroying all the subtle ones.

When this path has become very strong at the end of its practice, this experience is called "the collectedness likened to adamantine" (vajropama-samādhi). It is through this collectedness that one enters upon the Vimuktimārga or the Path of Freedom and thus becomes an Arhat.

THE SILENT BUDDHAS' VEHICLE

(Pratyekabuddhayāna)

The way of practice for one who desires to become a Silent Buddha (lit: a Buddha for oneself, that is one who cannot communicate his enlightenment to others), is very similar to the above, also having five paths as do the disciples. The differences here are that merit must be accumulated for a longer period to ensure this attainment, while the realization of enlightenment is centered about the penetration of Dependent Arising rather than of the Four Noble Truths.

THE GREAT VEHICLE

(Mahāyāna)

This is so called because one sets out with the idea to rid all beings of the stains. This Great Vehicle is divided into two sorts according to practice: the Vehicle of the Perfections (pāramitāyāna)[84] and the Adamantine Vehicle (vajrayāna). The latter will be dealt below under a separate heading while here we shall describe in brief the former which, like the Disciples' Vehicle, has five paths:

Sambhāramārga, the Path of Accumulation begins from the arising of the bodhicitta, or the mind determined to gain enlightenment, of which the cause is compassion (karuṇā). It is manifest in a strong desire to free beings from suffering. In one who experiences it, arises the desire to take upon his own shoulders the

Lord Buddha — a scroll painting

burden of leading all beings to freedom:[85] for the fulfillment of this aspiration such a noble person wishes to attain Buddhahood. This desire, devoid of all pretence, to become eventually a Buddha, is called the bodhicittotpāda (the arising of the bodhi-mind). After one has had this experience, one is called a bodhisattva (a being determined to attain bodhi). In the world one may also be known as a great being (mahāsattva), a Son of the Conquerors, and so forth, then becoming worthy to be worshipped by all celestials and men. As soon as the bodhicitta arises, one enters upon the Path of Accumulation in which manifold merits are gathered[86] and many of the mental stains become tranquil. This accumulation path is of three kinds, that is to say: weak, medium and strong. When this path is strong, one attains the accomplished stages of all the absorptions and thus comes to possess various psychic powers and superknowledges (ṛddhi, abhijñā). Since he possesses these, it is easy for the bodhisattva to move about among the various Buddha-lands (buddhakṣetra), in fact to go wherever he wishes to pay homage to the innumerable Buddhas teaching Dharma.[87] Again, when this path is strong, a bodhisattva attains a special kind of collectedness called śrotānugata through the power of which he is able to go to the different Buddha-lands and there listen to the deep and detailed teachings, afterwards being able to practice accordingly. In this strength of the accumulation path, a bodhisattva also obtains a thorough understanding of all dharmas.

Prayogamārga, the Path of Endeavor. When the bodhisattva achieves the perfection of both calm and insight which have the void as their object, this path is attained. The four aids to penetration, such as are found in the Disciples' path, are also to be found here. In these four—heat, summits, patience and sublime dharmas—he gradually advances while insight into voidness becomes progressively clearer and the dualism of subject and object begins to disappear, conceptualization about it becoming ever weaker. By his endeavor to practice in all his waking hours, both wisdom and skillful means (prajñā-upāya), the bodhisattva does not have the vision of the dharmas as substantial, even in his dreams. In whatever state he sees them, he perceives that they are insubstantial, that they are not an ātman. With this insight, he develops the desire to teach the Dharma to all beings. Reaching the summits (mūrdhana), a bodhisattva becomes competent to destroy the hindrances of four kinds arising as natural calamities due to the action of the four great elementals (earth, water, fire, air),[88] together with diseases and misfortunes. He is also able to pacify beings who bring harm upon others.[89] His speech also becomes accomplished, meaning that having spoken, he is able to pacify all obstacles. After the achievement of the Path of Endeavor, the enlightenment of the wise bodhisattva is assured, that is, he becomes irreversible and cannot then fall away from Dharma. There are certain signs experienced by him at this time, these being known as the avaivartikaliṅga (the marks of irreversibility) and he has such wondrous virtues as go beyond description.

The third path, that of insight, Darśanamārga, arises after the experience of the sublime dharmas (agradharma) when there is an unobstructed realization of voidness. In this path there are also found the two divisions of attainment (samāhita) and of bringing back to practice in daily life (pṛṣṭhalabdha), while the first is further divided into two, the anantarīyamārga, that is the path which "follows with no interval" upon the Path of Endeavor and the sublime dharmas, and second, the vimukti-mārga or the Path of Freedom. In the former, stains are destroyed and by the latter this attainment of freedom is held. In this path the stains destroyed are of two kinds respectively, the obstructions of stains and of knowledge. One who has practiced to the level of this path is free from the effects of karma as well as from defilement by the stains and thus freed from the duhkha usually connected with birth and death. As a result of this one attains a kind of collectedness known as sarvadharma-sukhaṃgama (all dharmas experienced as happiness), where all unpleasant feelings are no longer experienced as such. The Ārya who has attained this collectedness does not suffer even from causes normally giving rise to great suffering such as fire, weapons or poison and is always able to feel happiness.[90]

The fourth path is the Path of Development, Bhāvanāmārga. In this path are found the ten levels through which a bodhisattva practices to gain, after the tenth, Perfect Enlightenment. They are as follows:

1.	pramuditā	...	the joyous
2.	vimalā	...	the pure
3.	prabhākarī	...	the light-maker
4.	arciṣmati	...	the radiant
5.	sudurjayā	...	the invincible
6.	abhimukhī	...	the turning towards
7.	dūraṃgamā	...	the far-ranging
8.	acalā	...	the unshakable
9.	sādhumatī	...	the beneficial
10.	dharmamegha	...	the cloud of Dharma.

The duration of time spent by a bodhisattva in each of these levels may be immense, living through countless lives in the course leading to Buddhahood. He has many opportunities to meet with great numbers of Buddhas and to listen to their teachings thus furthering his advance through these levels. During this long period he ripens people for enlightenment by means of the four bases of sympathy: giving, kindly speech, beneficial conduct and impartiality[91] (dāna, priyavākya, artha-kriyā, samānārthatā). Each of the levels has its own special marks which, however, in this introductory work, we shall not elaborate. Suffice it to say that with advancement the virtues acquired become greater and ever superior. To gain a clear idea of these powers is really beyond the range of thought. Eventually, after advancing through all the levels, a bodhisattva attains to the cloud of Dharma in which the stream of even the most subtle obstructions to knowledge is cut off by the vajropama-samādhi, the collectedness likened to adamantine. This is the last stage of becoming and going beyond this a bodhisattva attains to Buddhahood. The virtues of a Buddha which are supreme and manifold will be discussed later.

THE ADAMANTINE VEHICLE

(Vajrayāna)

This vehicle is far superior to that of the perfections discussed above although the aims of both are the same, that is, the attainment of Buddhahood and in this ultimate attainment there can be no difference. But a great difference is to be found between these two vehicles regarding the skillful-means used for the attainment of Buddhahood.

When one considers the two aspects of the Buddha-body resulting from practice of the Adamantine vehicle, this difference becomes clear. These two aspects are called the Dharmakāya (truth-body) and Rūpakāya (form-body) and while both vehicles agree as the cause for former, there is some difference regarding the latter. The Dharmakāya has as its specific cause the wisdom found in the bodhicitta which penetrates to voidness, and this is also the supporting cause for the production of the Rūpakāya. Regarding the specific cause of the latter, however, there is a fundamental difference since Pāramitāyāna holds that this is simply the result of the bodhicitta and the accumulation of the six perfections,[92] while Vajrayāna attributes it to profound skillful means (gambhīrupāya). Since there is this difference in the skillful means employed, in Pāramitāyāna the course of practice to the attainment of Buddhahood requires effort applied in an immense number of lives spanning aeons of time and thus, according to this vehicle, it would be impossible to become a Buddha in one life time. But in Vajrayāna if one has a good teacher and if one's faculties are ripe, one can within a few years of effort, gain Buddhahood.[93]

The specific cause, as we said above, of the Rūpakāya is, according to Vajrayāna, the profound skillful means which are accomplished with the aid of devayoga[94] in the four grades of Tantra.[95] These four are graded according to the dull or sharp intelligence of those to be trained, further subdivisions being made, while the actual ways of training prescribed are innumerable. Their nature, formulation and the ways of explaining them, together with their various modes of fruiting all vary according to the person to be trained and the faculties possessed. The details of these ways of training are explained privately by a teacher to disciples accepted by him.[96] These disciples have had their minds mature by the performance of a consecration ceremony (abhiṣekha), thereby entering the circle of those who practice the Adamantine Vechicle. As this consecration and practice is of a personal nature, we are not going to explain these things here and what follows is only the briefest summary of Vajrayāna practice. (Because of the close relationship here between the teacher and his disciples, details cannot be given.)

The person who wants to practice the way of Tantric instructions should first be endowed with detachment and renunciation which is the common basis for all ways of practice in Buddha-dharma.[97] Such a person should also be endowed with the bodhicitta.[98] Well prepared in himself, he goes then to a teacher who is possessed of all the marks of competence[99] and humbly requests him for consecration and initiation into the circle of his disciples practicing the Vajrayāna. *Having received the consecration, he should observe well all the precepts for it is only upon the basis of virtuous conduct (śīla) that one can advance along the path.*[100]

While practicing the path of Tantras, one should pay special attention, firstly, to avabhāsa-pakṣa and secondly, to sunyatā-pakṣa. The first, which can be translated as the "wing of effulgence," means the mind becoming one-pointed upon the pictured form of the celestial being[101] whose practice one has taken up. Through this, one achieves the Rūpakāya of a Buddha. The second, called the "wing of voidness" is the experience of seeing nothing except the void. This is a very special stage when one experiences enlightenment and is also known as Mahāmudra (the Great Symbol). For the mind to remain fixed in this state one must take the special help of skillful means (upāya) whereby one knows the channels (of spiritual force, nāḍi) and the "winds" (the spiritual forces themselves, prāṇa). Through this knowledge and practice one achieves the Dharmakāya of a Buddha.

Equipped with these two wings one is thus as a bird flying through space, winging one's way to Buddhahood.

THE BODIES OF A BUDDHA

(*Buddha-kāya*)

AS I have said in the foregoing sections, the fruit of Buddhahood is attained by means of the path shown in the Sūtras and in the Tantras. In this section I have only given an outline of the meaning of Buddhahood regarding the various bodies used by Buddhas, while in the following section an account is given of the virtues (guṇa) of a Buddha's mind, speech and body.

The bodies of a Buddha are four in number and will be explained here in the following order:[102]

svabhāvakāya	...	self-existing-body
dharmakāya	...	dharma, or truth-body
sambhogakāya	...	enjoyment-body
nirmāṇakāya	...	created-body.

The svabhāvakāya may be considered under two aspects which help us to understand also the nature of the Dharmakāya. These are called the āgantukā-viśuddha-dharmakāya and the svabhāva-viśuddha-dharmakāya. The first of these is the pure Dharma-body (gained by the destruction of) the adventitious stains, while the second may be translated as the pure self-existing

Dharma-body. Regarding the first one, it has already been related that in the tenth level, called the cloud of Dharma, the collectedness likened to adamantine arises, by means of which are destroyed for ever all the obstructions to profound knowledge (jñeyāvaraṇa). Immediately, there is experienced the entrance into Vimuktimārga, the Path of Freedom, in which there are no obstructions by the stains (kleśāvaraṇa) remaining to be destroyed. Both of these kinds of obstructions are called adventitious taints (āgantukamala) and when they have been destroyed one attains to āgantuka-viśuddha-dharmakāya.

The minds of beings are, in reality, always void, being really not-self-nature. This natural voidness of the mind is variously called " the lineage of the self-existent," "the lineage of the Buddhas," "the seed of the Buddhas," or " the womb of the Tathāgatas," this last name being found in many Mahāyāna scriptures. This Buddha lineage exists in the minds of all beings and it is for this reason that all beings are able (given suitable conditions) to attain to Buddhahood.

After practicing, when a bodhisattva attains the ultimate stage when the mind is free from adventitious taints, then the knowledge of not-self-nature becomes clear to him, this being called svabhāva-viśuddha-dharmakāya. This cannot be found in the false state of mind in which the adventitious stains are always arising but is seen only in the stage of Buddhahood attainment. It is not impermanent, not created by causes and effects, is uncompounded and therefore never-changing.

To see clearly all dharmas which can be known both with the eye of relative truth and with that of Absolute Truth, is called the Dharmakāya, also known as the all-knowing knowledge (sarvajña-jñāna). Although it is one and not manifold yet it can be viewed in many ways, for instance from the viewpoint of the thirty-seven wings of enlightenment,[103] or in the light of the group of twenty-one unpolluted knowledges (anāśrava-jñāna-varga—see below in virtues of the Buddha-mind).

Now we come to the explanation of the enjoyment-body (Sambhogakāya). I have already said that there are ten levels through which a bodhisattva passes. From the eighth level called the "unshaken," onwards, there is a special sort of development and the perfections practiced on these levels are called the endeavor for the Pure Land (kṣetra-pariśuddhi-prayoga). By this practice there is the attainment of the body and the place of birth of the future Buddha. The levels from the eighth to the tenth are called the pure levels (viśud-dha-bhūmi) because in these levels the mind does not grasp at self-natureness. This practice is the primary cause of the enjoyment body, the skillful roots being ripened to ensure its place of birth. The Sambhoga-kāya is manifest in akaniṣṭhaghana-vyūhakṣetra (the cloud-array of the Greatest Ones' Land) and a bodhi-sattva's attainment of Buddhahood takes place first in this land. In this state of Buddhahood there are five fixed dharmas, that is to say, the place, body, retinue, the Dharma taught by him, and the time, all are very sure. The Sambhogakāya arises only in this land

and for this reason it is said that the place is fixed. Then the fixity of body means that it possesses the thirty-two major and the eighty minor marks of a great person. By fixed retinue is meant that only noble bodhisattvas are found there, while fixity of Dharma means that they always teach the Great Vehicle. As long as the wandering-on (saṃsara) exists, they show no changes in their body, such as those of old age, death and so forth. The body endowed with these five fixed dharmas is called the "enjoyment-body" and further, it is the basis for the "created-body."

This is called the Nirmāṇakāya and is not possessed of the five fixed dharmas but may be seen by ordinary men. Three aspects of it are distinguished:

uttama-nirmāṇakāya,
śailpika-nirmāṇakāya, and
nairyāṇika-nirmāṇakāya.

The first of these, the highest created-body, is directly related to the enjoyment-body. Having been born in different worlds such as Jambūdvīpa,[104] this first aspect also possesses the major and minor marks of a great person, as indeed did the Śākyamuni. Also, there occurs in the life of a Buddha, twelve great events bringing welfare to men who can be trained. These twelve are as follows:[105]

i departure from the Tuṣita celestial world of the bodhisattva who spends his last but one life there,

ii entering the womb of the royal mother during which she dreams of a white elephant with six tusks descending from the skies, iii birth from the right side of the queen while she is standing in the park at Lumbini, outside Kapilavastu,

iv education in which the young bodhisattva-prince astonishes his teachers with his immense fund of knowledge,

v enjoyment of royal estate in the palaces surrounded by everything beautiful and unblemished,

vi progress through Kapilavastu seeing old age, disease, death and a religious mendicant, and being stirred by these, going forth to homelessness,

vii practice of austerity for six years on the banks of the river Nairañjara near Gaya,

viii going to the bodhi-tree and sitting there (at the spot known as the Adamantine Seat (vajrāsana, at Buddha Gaya),

ix complete subjection of Māra (the personification of evil) at that place,

x attainment there of perfect enlightenment on the Full Moon of Vaiśākha (usually April-May),

xi turning the Wheel of Dharma for the first time (at the deer park outside Benares) to teach the five ascetics on the eve of the Full Moon of Āṣāḍha (the second full moon after Vaiśākha),

xii the Mahāparinirvāṇa, the "great entire quenching," (at Kuśinārā). All these are counted as acts of Lord Buddha although actually the first two are events from his previous life as a bodhisattva.

The second aspect of the created-body, the śailpika-nirmāṇakāya, is a specially created and supremely fashioned form. An example of this occurs in the story of the proud gandharva or celestial minstrel whom Śākyamuni subdued by showing himself as a lute-master.[106]

The nairyāṇika-nirmāṇakāya or the third aspect of the created-body means that a Buddha may be born in the form of other beings as when for instance, Lord Buddha prior to his birth as son of king Śuddhodana was born as a celestial being in Tusita by the name of Sacchavetaketu.[107]

Of the above four bodies, Svabhāvakāya and Dharmakāya cannot be seen by ordinary trainable men whereas the Saṃbhogakāya and the Nirmaṇakāya can be perceived by them according to their merits and it is therefore these last two which are immediately for the benefit of the world.

The four bodies may be thought of as three if the Svabhāvakāya and the Dharmakāya are collectively called just Dharmakāya, while these three can be still further reduced to two by combining Saṃbhogakāya and Nirmāṇakāya and considering both of them as Rūpakāya (form-body).

THE VIRTUES OF A BUDDHA

(Buddhaguṇa)

NOW a Buddha, in the aspect of the form-body, has numerable virtues but all of them can be gathered under four headings: those of body, speech, mind and karma. In the account below I shall only explain them in brief.

Bodily Virtues. The thirty-two marks of a great person such as the golden wheel on the instep of the foot, and the eighty minor marks, for instance the nails red like copper, are among the bodily virtues. By the sight of the body decorated with them, the roots for enlightenment can be established in beings. The bodily form of unenlightened beings, which is a "with-pollutions-heap" (sāśraya-skandha), does not have the thirty-two or the eighty marks which comprise a form embodying all-knowledge (sarvajñatā). Each one of these marks, even to each hair, can penetrate to true knowledge of every knowable object.

Besides, a Buddha can display various kinds of bodily manifestations in the various world systems. In one

Buddhafield he may go to birth, in another set rolling the Wheel of Dharma, in yet another show himself pursuing the bodhisattva career, while in a fourth he may be seen attaining the " great entire quenching," and it is through such deeds that trainable beings are established in the true path. It is said that Buddhas can show the bodies and deeds of all the Buddhas of the past, present and future in each pore of their bodies, also displaying the whole procession of their own lives while a bodhisattva in every single pore.

Verbal Virtues. A Buddha's speech is called gentle, appealing and beneficial because it gives rise to and develops the roots of skill according to the capacity of individual beings.[108] It is called mild because by listening to that speech the mind is permeated by joy. Also, it is called knowledgeable speech because by means of it, the twofold truth, Dependent Arising and so forth, are established. Again, it is said to be mind-delighting because it expresses the Dharma clearly. In this way there are sixty-four virtues pertaining to a Buddha's speech which are called collectively, brahmasvāra, the Divine Sound, and are found in every speech, sentence and word. The greatest special characteristic is that while a Buddha is teaching, celestials, serpent-beings and demons, celestial minstrels and all the tribes of men understand him in their own language. These are some of the virtues of a Buddha's speech.

Mental Virtues. Primarily, these are of two kinds, those connected with wisdom and those with compassion. As we related above under the Dharmakāya section, there are twenty-one unpolluted knowledges among which, however, some are shared by the Disciples and Silent Buddhas, those remaining being peculiar to perfectly Enlightened Ones. Here, passing over those common to the enlightenment of the former two, we shall discuss only those possessed by the Perfect Buddhas. Firstly, there are a Buddha's **Ten Powers** (daśabala).[109]

I. 1 sthānāsthāna-jñāna: this knowledge is knowing the causes producing an arisen phenomenon (sthāna) as well as the causes which do not produce a particular thing (asthāna).

2 karmavipāka-jñāna: by means of this knowledge a Buddha knows skillful, unskillful (kuśala, akuśala) and other groups of karma together with their results, as they are committed by, and then as they affect, those engaging in them.

3 dhyāna-vimokṣādi-jñāna: this knowledge arises to a Buddha who has taken the form and formless absorptions as his basis thus coming to know the most subtle differences of the various stages and freedoms.

4 indriya-parāpara-jñāna: through this knowledge a Buddha knows the sharp, medium and dull faculties of trainable beings.

5 nānādimukti-jñāna: of these different beings to be trained, a Buddha knows by means of this knowledge, their individual inclinations influenced by greed, aversion and delusion.

6 aṣṭādaśa-dhātuprabhedādi-jñāna: a Buddha knows the analysis of dharmas into the eighteen elements by means of this knowledge (see heaps, entrances and elements).

7 bhava-samasarvatragāmini-pratipad-jñāna: from the lowest levels of the states of deprivation (apāya-bhūmi) up to the summit of existence (bhavāgra) there are many levels called "bhūmi" while beyond this becoming lies the realm and freedom of the Āryas, and of all this, mundane and super-mundane, a Buddha has knowledge.

8 purva-nivāsānusmṛti-jñāna: through this knowledge the Buddhas know the past lives of beings.

9 cyutyupapatti-jñāna: the death and birth of beings according to their karma is known by a Buddha through this knowledge.

10 āśravakṣāya-jñāna: a Buddha has neither the obstruction of stains nor that of knowledge and thus knows his own and others' destruction of the pollutions (āśrava, of sensuality, existence, unknowing and of views), both now and in the future.

II. Another important group of mental virtues are the **Four Confidences of a Buddha:** (catur-vaiśāradya).[110] Regarding these, a Buddha during his teaching or in any bodily or verbal action has perfect confidence without any hesitation or fear of criticism and is for this reason called "possessor of supreme confidence," (vaiśāradya-prāpta). As in the case of our Lord Buddha, there are four declarations which a Buddha makes with supreme confidence from which are derived this list of four confidences:

1 sarva-dharmābhi-sambodhi-pratijñā-vaiśāradya: Lord Buddha proclaimed: "I have penetrated to enlightenment in respect of all dharmas," and declaring this does not fear any reasonable condemnation from others wishing to refute him.

2 sarvāśravakṣāya-jñāna-pratijñā-vaiśāradya: Lord Buddha proclaimed: "I have attained the destruction of all the pollutions," and in declaring this he does not fear any reasonable condemnation from others wishing to refute him.

3 antarāyika-dharmavyākaraṇa-pratijñā-vaiśāradya: Lord Buddha proclaimed: "I have announced obstructing dharmas (such as greed, aversion and delusion) to be obstructions," and in declaring this he does not fear any reasonable condemnation from others wishing to refute him.

4 nairyāṇikapratipadvyākaraṇa-pratijñā-vaiśāradya: Lord Buddha proclaimed: "I have announced (the perfect understanding of the Four Noble Truths as) the practice-path leading out (of duhkha to Nirvāṇa). Lord Buddha expounded this way out of compassion for all trainable beings. Declaring this he did not fear any

reasonable condemnation from others wishing to refute him.

III. Another group of mental virtues are called the three **Unconfused Awarenesses** (asambhinna-smṛtyupasthāna) [111] meaning that while teaching Lord Buddha had a mind unconfused in three respects:

1 śuśrūṣamāneṣu-samacittatā: Lord Buddha while teaching had a mind of evenness (with no attachment) toward those disciples who listen respectfully and with trust in their hearts.

2 aśuśrūṣamāneṣu-samacittatā: for those not listening respectfully and with no trust, Lord Buddha has also evenness-mind (with no dislike present).

3 śuśrūṣāśuśrūṣamāneṣu-samacittatā: when teaching a mixed audience of those listening well and those not attentive, in Lord Buddha no liking could arise for the former and no dislike for the latter, there being just the maintenance of the mind of evenness.

IV. Then again, there is the group of the three **Unhidden Dharmas** (agupta-dharma).[112] As Lord Buddha has done nothing through the doors of body, speech or mind which was blameable, so he had no thought to hide anything done by himself with the idea, "May others not know of this." His actions through the three doors being quite open and unconcealed, these are called the three unhidden Dharmas.

V. The **Absence of Forgetfulness** (nāsti-muṣitā) is another of the mental virtues. This means that Lord Buddha always remembers the persons, times and places when beings may be helped and having this knowledge, he approaches them at the right time and place, speaking Dharma in appropriate words.

VI. Another sort of mental virtue which should be mentioned is called: samyak pratihāta-vāsanatvā, meaning that in the mind of a Buddha, all the tendencies (vāsanā) pertaining to the two sorts of obstructions (āvaraṇa) are completely destroyed.

VII. Mahākaruṇā or the **Great Compassion** means that in the Buddha-mind only the thought, "Whom can I tame and establish upon the right way" (of perfect understanding) is entertained.

VIII. Now we should consider a very important group of dharmas known as the eighteen **Special Virtues of a Buddha** (āveṇika-buddhaguṇa). These are not found either in disciples or in the Silent Buddhas but are peculiar to the Perfect Buddhas. Among them there are four categories, such that six fall under the category of conduct (caryā), six under enlightenment (bodhi), three under karma while the last three refer to knowledge (jñāna).

1 nāsti-tathāgatasya-skhalitam: for the Tathāgata there is no fear from robbers, animals, etc. whether he lives in the city or in the forest.

2 nāsti-ravitam: A Buddha does not laugh or complain upon such occasions as taking the right road, or upon losing the way. He makes no childish noises or exclamations.

3 nāsti-muṣitāsmṛtitā: He never forgets which things are to be done, neither their time nor their place, accomplishing all at the right time.

4 nāsti-asamāhitacittam: Whether he has entered into the absorptions or not, his mind is always well established in voidness.

5 nāsti-nānātva-saṃjñā: He does not perceive the difference between the perverted quality of saṃsāra and the peacefulness of Nirvāṇa, not conceptualizing in this matter.

6 nāsti-apratisaṃkhyopekṣā: He is not thoughtlessly indifferent to teaching when the appropriate place, time and person are present.

The above six special dharmas fall in the category of conduct.

7 nāsti-chandahāniḥ: He wishes always that the rain of his friendliness and compassion should fall steadily and continuously upon suffering beings.

8 nāsti-vīryahāniḥ: although Buddha-lands are as numerous as sand-grains by the Ganges, still Buddhas are so energetic that if there is but one person to be benefitted, one of them will go to give his aid without any decrease of his energy.

9 nāsti-smṛtihāniḥ: He is always able to remember the workings of the minds of others and know the correct skillful means (upāya) for establishing them on the way, thus showing that a Buddha suffers no decrease of memory power.

10 nāsti-samādhihāniḥ: He has a mind forever well concentrated and established in the essence of all dharmas (voidness). By reason of this virtue he is never separated from this penetration to the nature of reality.

11 nāsti-prajñāhāniḥ: in beings there are many kinds of stains for the destruction of which a Buddha out of his wisdom expounds the 84,000 sections of Dharma. Although he expounds these Dharma-sections, his wisdom is not depleted thereby.

12 nāsti-vimuktihāniḥ: A Buddha has attained the freedom in which there is the cessation of all obstructions and he can never fall from this state of freedom:

These six special dharmas belong to the Bodhi category.

13 kāya-karma: spreading rays of light from the body and the constant mindfulness of the four positions (īryāpatha)—walking, standing, sitting, lying—constitute the bodily karma of a Buddha.

14 vāk-karma: knowing the different inclinations of beings, a Buddha speaks Dharma accordingly. This is the speech-karma of a Buddha.

15 cittakarma: the mental karma of a Buddha is the continual dwelling in friendliness and compassion. The above three dharmas specially pertain to karma.

16-18 The last three concern a Buddha's unobstructed penetration into the dharmas of the past, present, and future without being attached to any of them. These three concerning knowledge of all the times are in the jñāna or knowledge category.

IX. The All knowing knowledge (sarvajñā-jñāna).[113] Here the word " sarva " signifies the heaps, entrances and elements since, apart from them, there is no other dharma to be found. A Buddha has knowledge of them directly, not by way of reflection or speculation. It is this which is called the all-knowing knowledge and, since he knows the All, he is called the All-knower. Regarding this knowledge he has unlimited and wonderful virtues, difficult indeed to describe rightly.

I said above that a Buddha's mental virtues were of two kinds: those pertaining to knowledge and those to compassion. Of the nine groups outlined above there are twenty-one virtues on the side of knowledge (all those in groups I, II, and III, plus the last three in VIII and IX). We now continue by explaining the Great Compassion.

From the Path of Accumulation up to the Collectedness like Adamantine of the Development-path, is just called the Path of Training (śaikṣamārga) because in all of these levels a bodhisattva needs training for his continuous advancement. While progressing on this Path of Training, a bodhisattva develops great compassion again and again, thus aiding both beings and his onward march to Buddhahood. With the full unfolding of this great compassion there is the attainment of perfect enlightenment for which reason Lord Buddha is called the " Greatly Compassionate One." This attainment is also called the Path of No-training (aśaikṣa-mārga), that is, where there is no longer effort needed for training. Compassion flows naturally and without effort when one enlightened has seen the sufferings of beings, which are indeed innumerable. Both beings and their manifold experiences of duhkha are too numerous to count, there being no limit to either as there is no limit to the sky. Whether in the past, now in the present, or among beings who will arise in the future, all have, do and will experience duhkha in some form or other. A Buddha, having known all these beings, makes them the object of his great compassion, always radiating this compassion effortlessly so that the world is benefited without obstructions.

Having now discussed three sorts of Buddha-virtues, we come now to the fourth and last group:

Karma-virtues. The supreme and special virtues of a Buddha's karma may be divided into two categories: nirābhoga-karma (not-considered karma) and avicchinna-karma (not-interrupted karma).

The first of these, literally "action which is not considered," really means that which is effortless or that action which is done according to the nature of circumstances. Although a Buddha is seen to exercise the four positions (of the body) and the psychic powers, yet he has no need to make an effort for these things. Nevertheless, their purpose is served as by seeing them, trainable men experience the arising of the bodhicitta.

In the mind of a Tathāgata, there does not arise the thought, "I shall teach this or that person, this kind or that sort of Dharma"[114] yet according to the inclinations of trainable men, many teachings flow out quite naturally. This is one special characteristic of this type of karma.

No thought arises in the mind of a Buddha suggesting that he should benefit beings in the world but because of the virtues of his great compassion he establishes men in the skillful roots and thereby benefits them in ways both mundane and supermundane. This is another special characteristic of his effortless karma.

It should be understood that when ordinary people make actions bodily or verbal, these are certainly preceded by thought leading to their accomplishment. Indeed, without such prior thought, no intentional actions of these sorts can be performed. Now for one who is practicing and making progress along the Path of Training, the amount of this prior consideration steadily decreases as one advances through the various levels. As far as the eighth level, such prior consideration is still to be found in a gross form but from the eighth to the tenth, gross reflections are calmed and no longer arise, as for instance when a bodhisattva is teaching others. Thus, the good of the world is achieved effortlessly in the last three levels though even there subtle considerations still linger before the accomplishment of bodily and verbal karmas, it being impossible therefore to call these " not considered." While the obstructions to knowledge (jñeyāvaraṇa) still persist, thoughts of a subtle kind will be found to precede action but when these obstructions have been destroyed completely upon the tenth level, then the flow of this not-considered karma has no longer anything to check it.

The second of the karma-virtues, called the uninterrupted, is so-called since a Buddha's actions flow without being cut off. In explanation of this we may consider the training from another point of view, that of the two burdens to be accumulated by a bodhisattva. These are the burden of merits and that of knowledge (punya-, and jñāna-sambhāra). Under the first burden are grouped five of the six perfections, while the sixth, the perfection of wisdom, constitutes the second burden. By means of the first burden of merits the form-body of a Buddha is achieved, while the second of knowledge leads to realization of the Dharma-body. From the steady accumulation of these burdens through the various levels, a bodhisattva comes to the attainment of Buddhahood after which there is a continuous flow of karma (from the infinite accumulated resources).

The mind-element (citta-dhātu), also called the tathāgata-womb (tathāgata-garbha) is by nature undefiled but is covered over with stains and their tendencies (kleśa, vāsanā) which are adventitious.[115] For this reason their destruction is possible, not impossible. From his great compassion, Lord Buddha has pointed out the ways and means whereby one may rid oneself of all the mentally defiling stains. This is the uninterrupted flow of the karma of Lord Buddha arising from out of his compassion.

Thus having briefly explained
the twofold Truth
the three Collections of Sacred Lore
the threefold Training,
the Path of Practice through the three Vehicles
and
the fourfold Buddha-body with its virtues,
We come to the conclusion.
May this book help to spread knowledge
of Lord Buddha's Dharma
to the four corners of the world
and may all people receive its benefits.

Finished the transcription of this book at Wat Bovoranives Vihāra, Bangkok, upon the auspicious day of Pavāraṇā (Admonition Day), on the Full Moon of Assayuja, 2509 years after the Great Parinibbāna.

(October 29, 1966)

NOTES TO THE TEXT

(Notes marked 'H' are translated from the Hindi edition.)

PAGE 12 (1) H. The examination of dharmas, events of sensory and mental experience, is itself wisdom and leads to greater wisdom (prajñā) so that experience is understood in terms of skillful, unskillful (kuśala, akuśala), worldly, superworldly (laukika, lokottara) and other points of opposites and classifications. When fully developed this wisdom is that which goes beyond (to Nirvāṇa) and is called Prajña-pāramitā. This is the wisdom of the Buddhas. It is Buddhist tradition to place upon the opening page of a book explaining Lord Buddha's teachings, such a salutation showing respect or the analytical understanding or wisdom which leads one to the beyond.

(2) H. ŚĪLA-KĀLA: The total duration of Gotama the Buddha's dispensation is said to be 5000 years. This has been divided by scholars into ten divisions each of 500 years:

i of those who practice Dharma many become Arhats, hence the name Arhat-time.

ii of those who practice Dharma many become Anāgāmi, hence the name Non-returners'-time.

iii of those who practice Dharma many become Śrota-āpanna, hence the name Stream-enterers'-time.

The above three comprising 1500 years are together called the Enlightenment-time (bodhi-kāla).

iv people generally possess much wisdom (prajñā): Wisdom-time.

v people generally possess much collectedness (samādhi): Collectedness-time.

vi people generally possess much virtue (śīla): Virtue-time. These three are called the time of striving (sādhana-kāla).

vii people are interested in the *Adhidharma*: Abhidharma time.

viii people are interested in the *Sūtra*: Discourse-time.

ix people are interested in the *Vinaya*: Discipline-time. These three are called the time of the scriptures (āgama-kāla).

x Jina-mātradhāraṇa: in this period learning and practice are nearly lost and people merely put on the signs of the holy life while leading an unworthy one.

(Although classifications of this sort are also found in Theravāda commentaries, they are not found in the Discourses of the Pāli Canon where the spirit is very much: " If one practices earnestly and correctly, one may attain to the highest," whatever age one is living in. For a similar Pāli work portraying the gradual decay of the teaching see the late (and non-canonical) *Anāgatavaṃsa* (Chronicle of the Future) partly translated in *Buddhist Texts*, edited by Dr. E. Conze.)

(3) H. In this Bhadrakalpa or Auspicious Aeon there will appear in Jambūdvīpa (rose-apple land, i.e. India, but originally meaning the southern continent in the ancient four-continents of old Indian geography), 1008 Buddhas in Created-body form (nirmāṇakāya). Before Gotama there were three, the Lords Krakucanda, Kanakamuni and Kāśyapa, the fourth being Gotama with 1004 thus to appear in future. (In Theravāda, this Auspicious Aeon will have five Buddhas: the three above being the Buddhas of the past, Gotama that of the present and Ariya Metteyya * who is still a bodhisattva in Tuṣita celestial realm, the only Buddha commonly named for the future. Other Pāli sources give the names of other Buddhas of the past and future but not of this aeon.)

Page 14 (4) DHARMA—a word with many meanings. From the root " dhṛ " which has the sense of upholding, Dharma is therefore that which upholds one's efforts when one practices in accordance with it. Dharma is Law, that is the Law governing the arising, existence and passing away of all physical and psychological phenomena. The Dharma is also the traditional way of naming the teaching of Lord Buddha.

(5) DUHKHA—a very important term. Often rendered as " suffering," it is then inadequate and we have preferred either the cumbersome but more accurate " unsatisfactoriness " or else to leave the term untranslated. Duhkha may be physical (pain)

* [Ārya Maitreya, Skt.]

or mental (anguish), it refers to the facts of " birth, old age, disease and death," to the common enough " grief, lamentation, pain, anguish and despair," to being " conjoined with what one does not like " and being " separated from what one likes, not to getting what one wants." The very components of our personality are, because we grasp at them (as " I," as " mine "), bound up with duhkha. " Duhkha should be understood " within one's " own " mind and body and when it is understood one will know true happiness. Phrases in parentheses in these notes are quoting the words of Lord Buddha.

Page 16 (6) The famous opening verses of the *Dhammapada*: " Events are heralded by mind, mind is chief, mind-made are they. . . ." The pre-eminence of mind is also well illustrated in the Wheel of Wandering-on (samsāracakra) where the mind is pictured as the oarsman in the boat while the body is just the passive passenger.

Page 17 (7) See MAHĀ-NIDĀNA-SUTTA, the Great Discourse on Causation, *Dīgha-nikāya* (Long Discourses of the Buddha), Sutta 14, under the explanation of feelings (vedanā).

Page 19 (8) See SABBĀSAVA-SUTTA, the Discourse on All Troubles, *Majjhima-nikāya* (Middle Length Sayings), Sutta 2.

Page 20 (9) SHAME AND FEAR OF BLAME: " Two clear things, O bhikkhus, protect the world. Which two? Shame and fear of blame. . .". (*Anguttara-nikāyā*, 11.7).

Page 22 (10) PUNARBHĀVA which means literally " again-becoming." This literal translation preserves the Buddhist emphasis upon dynamic and changing psychological states, a psychology which operates without reference to hypothetical static entities such as soul, atman, etc. " Reincarnation " is a term quite foreign to Buddhist psychology since it presupposes that which is to incarnate again. Even rebirth is only used for clarity of expression (one only finds " birth " " jāti " mentioned in the texts) but for depth of meaning " again-becoming " is much to be preferred.

Page 23 (11) The four great elementals (mahābhūta) are earth, water, fire and air, or as the ancient commentaries characterize them: solidity, cohesion, temperature and movement.

Page 24 (12) SABHĀVAVĀDA " the doctrine that the universe was produced and is sustained by the natural and necessary action of substances according to their inherent properties and not by the agency of a supreme being." (Apte's Sanskrit Dictionary.)

(13) See MAHĀKAMMAVIBHAṄGA SUTTA, the Great Discourse on the Analysis of Kamma, *Majjhima-nikāya* (Middle Length Sayings), Sutta 136: The view founded upon incomplete knowledge that " Indeed everyone (committing the ten evil and unskillful actions) after dying arises in good bourn. . . ."

Page 25 (14) Two or three volumes written by a Hindu yogi under the title *Experiences of a Yogi* (published in Ahmedabad, Gujarat, India) give a good modern illustration of this. The author evidently, from his descriptions, had practiced up to the absorptions of form and formlessness (rūpa- and arūpa-dhyāna) and finding no ultimate freedom which was irreversible, he despaired of finding it at all, declaring that no such state existed.

Page 26 (15) literally, every mind (citta) arises from another mind (citta) but better translated here as " mental state."

(16) three theories are here invalidated: ahetuka-vāda, īśvara-nirmāṇahetu and the ideas of the Indian Materialists, the Cārvāka.

(17) See *Aṅguttara-nikāya*, I. 5. 9-10: " This mind, O bhikkhus, is luminous but is defiled (in the common man) by adventitious stains. This mind, O bhikkhus, is luminous and is freed (in the noble disciple) of the adventitious stains."

Page 27 (18) as when the Cārvāka avers that insects are born out of dirt. Compare with the mediaeval western belief that mushrooms were magically produced, or the old gardeners' belief that potato-blight is caused by thunderstorms.

Page 28 (19) There is also the technique of hypnotic regression. See also *Twenty Cases Suggestive of Re-incarnation* (Proceedings of American Psychical Research Society, 1966) of Dr. Ian Stevenson of the Virginia School of Medicine, and of Mr. Francis Story's, *The*

Case for Rebirth, Wheel Publications, Nos. 12-13, Buddhist Publication Society, Kandy, Ceylon.

Page 30 (20) Every form of Buddhist teaching offers two ways of practice. One aims at the slow accumulation of merits through many lives until, in the distant future, Nirvāṇa is attained. This is illustrated in Tibetan tradition by the Vehicle of the Perfections and the way advocated by the Mahāyāna Sūtras (most of them). In Theravāda, much the same tradition is seen in the practice of lay-people (and of some bhikṣus) who are encouraged to make merit for the attainment of good future births. Difference can only be seen here if first the Perfections are completely altruistically performed (difficult to find) and if merit is accumulated selfishly (but it is often dedicated to all beings in Theravāda lands). The other way is the direct attack upon the problems of ignorance and craving more often taken up by monastic disciples (though of course lay-people are by no means debarred from this). This corresponds in Tibetan to the Vajrayāna techniques of meditation whereby one becomes a siddha (accomplished one) in this life. See examples of this in the lives of the Mahāsiddha Naropa and of Jetsun Milarepa. Theravāda tradition also stresses very strongly the direct approach, for among Lord Buddha's words preserved in the Suttas are frequently found exhortations addressed to (mostly) bhikṣus urging them to the attainment of one of the noble fruits (āryaphala) in this very life. While the practicers of the Tantras cultivate seclusion on hills and mountains, the earnest practicer in Theravāda went, and still goes, to the jungle. Modern Theravāda meditation teachers have the same approach. Note for instance, the remark of the late Ven. Chao Khun Upāli (Siricando): " If a Buddhist cannot at least become a Stream-enterer in this very life, he can indeed be said to have wasted his entire existence."

Page 32 (21) See *Sutta Nipāṭa*, verses 885-6. To the question, ". . . is truth many and at variance?" Lord Buddha replies: " Truth, verily, is not many nor at variance." Lord Buddha also declares, (verse 884): " Truth is one without a second."

Page 34 (22) This fault has been added by the venerable translator of the Hindi edition, for which he quotes as source the *Āryabhisandhinirmocana Sūtra*.

Page 35 (23) THERAVĀDA scholastic tradition regards the seeing of the real nature of the dharmas as belonging to Absolute Truth since such seeing must be accomplished by insight (vipaśyanā). However, more practical sources in Theravāda, that is the meditation teachers, instruct that one should not get entangled with the intricacies of commentaries and sub-commentaries but rather investigate the dharmas in one's " own " mental-material continuity. Note the *Dhammapada*: All dhammas are anattā (not-self-soul and therefore void).

Page 36 (24) [No notes given in original ed.]

Page 38 (25) AVIJÑAPTI-RŪPA: Dr. E. Conze in his *Buddhist Thought in India* (Allen and Unwin), p. 181, has this to say about this somewhat complex subject: " This is a term for the hidden imprints on our bodily structure which are brought about by such actions as committing a murder, taking up the disciplines, performing dhyāna, or viewing the truth on the Path. They make a man into a different kind of person, and continue to grow until their reward or punishment is reached. An act of will may manifest itself externally and materially in gestures and words. At the same time a good or bad action for which a person is responsible may result in an unmanifested and invisible modification of a person's material structure—for instance, if he arranges for someone to be killed without contributing to the killing by either words or overt deeds."

(26) SAMSKĀRAS associated with consciousness:

11 present in all consciousness (mahābhūmika-dharma)
10 skillful qualities (kuśala-mahābhūmika-dharma)
6 stained qualities (kleśa-mahābhūmika-dharma)
2 unskillful qualities (akuśala-mahābhūmika-dharma)
10 limited unskillful qualities (upakleśa-paritta-bhūmika-dharma)
8 indeterminate (aniyata-bhūmika-dharma).

Saṃkāras dissociated from consciousness:

14 Saṃskāras which are immaterial but not associated with consciousness.

They include: possession, non-possession, birth, continuance, decay and impermanence.

For the fully-developed scheme in Theravāda Abhidhamma see the *Abhidhammaṭṭhasaṅgaha* (various translations in English).

Page 42 (27) TWELVEFOLD TEACHING (dvādaśāṅga-śāsana):

i Sūtra: the word of Lord Buddha in prose which could be easily understood.
ii Geyya: prose sayings interspersed with verses.
iii Vyākaraṇa: expositions by learned bhikṣus of brief discourses given by Lord Buddha.
iv Gāthā: verse and metrical sayings such as *Dhammapada*, etc.
v Udāna: inspired utterances including the *Udāna* book.
vi Itiyukta: sayings opening with "For it has been said," including the *Itiyukta* book, (Pāli: *Itivuttaka*).
vii Jātaka: birth stories of the bodhisattva to become Lord Buddha, such as Viśvantara, Mahāgovindiya, Sudarśana.
viii Adbhutadharma: marvellous and wonderful qualities events, etc. related in some Sūtras.
ix Vaidalya: subtle analyses imparted by particularly well-developed disciples. Mahāyāna Sūtras have been included under this heading. Theravāda knows the above nine aṅgas (in Pāli: Sutta, Geyya, Veyyākaraṇa, Gāthā, Udāna, Itivuttaka, Jātaka,

Abbhutadhamma, Vedalla). The remaining three are found in Sarvāstivāda and Mahāyāna:

x Nidāna: introductory material before a discourse.

xi Avadāna: legends of the previous lives of great disciples (see Pāli, Apadāna).

xii Upadeśa: instruction on profound and mysterious dharmas. The Vajrayāna Tantras have been included under this heading.

Page 43 (28) THE FOUR NOBLE TRUTHS (Āryasatya):

The Truth of Unsatisfactoriness (duhkha)
The Truth of the Origination of duhkha
The Truth of the Cessation of duhkha
The Truth of the Practice-path leading to the cessation of duhkha.

DEPENDENT ARISING (Pratītya-samutpāda):

"Ignorance conditions karma-formations,
Karma-formations condition consciousness,
Consciousness conditions mentality-materiality,
Mentality-materiality conditions the six entrances,
Six entrances condition contact,
Contact conditions feeling,
Feeling conditions craving,
Craving conditions grasping,
Grasping conditions becoming,
Becoming conditions birth,
Birth conditions old age, death, grief, lamentation, pain, anguish, and despair. Thus arises this whole mass of duhkha again in the future."

(29) H. SVALAKṢAṆA (individual characteristic) has various meanings—a characteristic which is peculiar to a particular thing, as heat is a special characteristic of fire. Or it may mean condition of existence independent of time and space. A thing's natural or independent characteristics are svalakṣaṇa, by denying which the truth of voidness is established. Sāmanya-lakṣaṇa has also more than one meaning. A characteristic common to all is a general characteristic, as is impermanence, etc. of all conditioned things.

Page 44 (30) One should carefully distinguish the sceptical attitude rooted in delusion (moha) and which is therefore a hindrance to practice, from the questioning and investigation of Dharma which is born of the second kind of wisdom, cintāmaya-prajñā, the reflection or thinking wisdom. The first obstructs and should therefore be overcome while the second is a great aid and should therefore be developed. Lord Buddha in the discourse to the Kālāmas of Kesaputta with great ability used investigation to overcome the barrier of the sceptical Kālāma people. See *Aṅguttara-nikāya*, III. 65, Book of the Threes.

(31) See *Dhammacakkappavattana Sutta*, The Turning of the Wheel of Dharma, the first instruction given by Lord Buddha to the five ascetics in the deer park at Isipaṭṭaṇa (Sārnath) near Benares. The Pāli recension is found in *Samyutta-nikāya*, V. 421-3, while a Sanskrit one is available in *Mahāvastu*, III. 331. Translations

of both are available from the Pali Text Society and the former from the Buddhist Publication Society.

(32) The COLLECTION OF VINAYA is primarily for those gone forth to homelessness so that these indulgences which contravene the discipline of bhikṣus, are permissable within the bounds of restraint to lay Buddhists. These bounds are the Five Precepts which they have undertaken voluntarily, and knowledge from their own experience of what is not skillful and stains the mind.

Page 45 (33) DOGMATIC BELIEF (abhinivesa—abhiniveṣa, Sanskrit) of two varieties are distinguished in Theravāda Abhidhamma: Dogmatic belief induced by craving (tanhābhinivesa) to the body as " belonging-to-me," and dogmatic belief induced by (wrong) views (diṭṭhābhinivesa—dṛṣṭābhiniveṣa, Sanskrit) which is belief in the existence of ātman, soul, etc. Ven. Ledi Sayadaw says in his *Vipassanā-dīpanī*: " Abhinivesa means belief. . . set in the mind as firmly and as immovably as doorposts, stone pillars, and monuments. . .". See edition of the Buddhist Publication Society.

Page 46 (34) see page 43, note 29.

Page 47 (35) Sometimes called HĪNAYĀNA which however is an unpleasant term with a rather dubious history so that it is better avoided wherever possible. Śrāvakayāna, the Disciples' Vehicle, is much better since the śrāvaka or great disciples of Lord Buddha, such as Ven. Sāriputra and Ven. Maudgalyāyana, are honored in all Buddhist Lands.

(36) This MAHĀYĀNA definition of the virtue-training is perfectly in accord with Theravāda principles. It is interesting to note that it is both a root-offence and an ordinary one for those who have taken the bodhisattva saṃvara-śīla, (the Bodhisattva's precepts of restraint), " to disparage the Śrāvakayāna " (and encourage others to learn Mahāyāna only). Superiority feeling resulting in disparagement is after all, pride or conceit (māna), a powerful mental stain.

(37) As specially explained by H. H. The Dalai Lama, the two types of collectedness mentioned here are: Gaganagañja (lit: " infinite storehouse "). From the first level (bhūmi) of a bodhisattva, he *may* have the power to provide through magical power whatever is needed by people as a result of this samādhi, but this power refers particularly to the tenth level. Sūraṅgama means " effective in destroying evil." Generally, this refers to the knowledge (jñāna) from the first to the tenth levels which is powerful in destroying mental stains, while before entering on the ten levels, this knowledge was weak. But particularly, it refers to the tenth level where this knowledge is very powerful and will destroy all mental stains.

Page 48 (38) See *Vinaya Piṭaka*, V. 164, where there is the same teaching in greater detail.

Page 49 (39) Three Vehicles (carrying beings to enlightenment). This is a distinctively Mahāyāna concept and not found in the Pāli Canon.

Page 50 (40) A Hindu yogin may light five fires to the north, south, east and west leaving room for himself to sit at the centre. He sits down at midday when the sun is at its zenith, this being the fifth fire, for the full accomplishment of this act of self-torture. Elsewhere, also, where love or fear and desire form the basis of morality, one also sees that unskill is used to enforce moral conduct.

Page 51 (41) They are: celestials (deva), titans (asura), men (manuṣya), hungry ghosts (preta) animals (tiryagyoni), and hell-wraiths (naraka-sattva). See notes 43 and 70.

Page 53 (42) It is important that one has a clear idea of what is meant by karma. One short and famous definition of Lord Buddha will suffice here. The karma of a Buddha has another meaning (q.v.). " O bhikkhus, I say that volition (intentional action) is karma." See *Aṅguttara-nikāya*, VI. 63.

(43) Apāya-Bhūmi, the states of woe or deprivation, which are three: hungry ghosts (preta), animals (tiryagyoni) and hell-wraiths (nirāyaka). These are not fanciful imaginations but represent experiences of those who have made unskill so strong within themselves that their minds are no longer human, and therefore sink down to experience states subhuman.

Page 54 (44) A similar analysis of precepts is found in Theravāda though the number of factors for each precept varies from three to five.

Page 55 (45) One should note however, that the dominance of one root does not exclude another. Thus both greed and aversion (which cannot be present together in one moment of consciousness) are based upon delusion and do not arise without it, while as they are the reflexes of each other, where one is found the other is sure to occur. They may, in fact, alternate rapidly in their dominance of consciousness giving the unpracticed observer the impression that they co-exist within the same moment. Analysis will reveal alternation. Mercy-killing will also be rooted in delusion. The acutal act of killing, whatever is the motive for it, is rooted in aversion without which, it is explained in Theravāda, life cannot be destroyed.

Page 57 (46) Upavasatha, the day recurring twice in the lunar month (the 14th day—Full Moon, and the 1st day—New Moon) when the *Prātimokṣa Sūtra* of the basic rules of discipline is recited by bhikṣus and the lay-people who observe the eight Upavasatha precepts for one day and night. Special teaching is given to the lay-people who often spend the day within the vihāra, listening to, reading about, or meditating upon Dharma. The lay-people on their part make special offerings (food and other necessities) to the bhikṣus upon these days.

Page 58 (47) This refers either to worldly or to supermundane attainments. A bhikṣu may boast with untruth of his attainment of a dhyāna or of the state of Arhat, etc. If he does so, he has committed the fourth offence of the Defeat (pārājika) category and can no longer be regarded as a bhikṣu, must disrobe and can never again in this life be reordained. Lay-people who lie in this way have just a very bad karma to experience.

Page 63 (48) IMMEDIACY-KARMA (ānantarika-karma) or that karma which brings about immediate destiny, such that at the time of death the doer is driven into a very painful subhuman rebirth experiencing one of the hells.

Page 64 (49) See the theories expounded at the opening of the *Sāmaññaphala Sutta* in the *Dīgha-nikāya,* Sutta 2. Particularly the views of Purāṇa Kassapa (akiriyavāda) and Ajita Kesakambalin (ucche-davāda).

Page 65 (50) In THERAVĀDA only two classes of people observe the precepts called Pātimokkha: The bhikṣus and bhikṣuṇis (monks and nuns). At the present time there are no bhikṣuṇis in Theravāda countries so that only bhikṣus practice the Pātimokkha. While some of these precepts are also observed by novices (samanera), the word " Pātimokkha " is never in Theravāda, used to cover either their precepts, or those of lay-people.

Page 66 (51) In THERAVĀDA the novice has ten precepts and also should observe the five rules concerning gross misconduct (the same as the first five saṅghādisesa rules for bhikṣus), plus the seventy-five rules of training (sekhiyavatta).

(52) In THERAVĀDA, bhikṣu-precepts number 227; 4 Pārājika, 13 Saṅghādisesa, 2 Aniyata, 30 Nissaggiya Pācittiya, 92 Pācittiya, 4 Pāṭidesanīya, 75 Sekhiya, 7 Adhikaraṇa-samatha.

(53) It should be clearly understood that the bhikṣu and bhikṣuṇi precepts, in fact all these Pātimokkha precepts, are derived from the Śrāvakayāna (of the Mūla-Sarvāstivāda school) and differ only in minor points from those in Theravāda. Tibetan bhikṣus are therefore Sarvāstivāda bhikṣus being Mahāyāna to the extent that they practice Mahāyāna ideals and learn Mahāyāna texts. *There is no Mahāyāna ordination as a bhikṣu* (but only as a bodhisattva). Bhikṣuṇis exist today in China (Taiwan), Korea and Vietnam.

Page 68 (54) The *Mahāmaṅgala Sutta* accounts these as among the highest blessings, that is: " samanānañca dassanaṃ—the seeing of samanas " (bhikṣus) and " kālena dhammasavanaṃ—hearing Dharma in due time."

Page 71 (55) Usually the term " citta " is translated as " mind " but it really means the total mental-emotional experience of which one is aware as well as that of which one is not aware. It embraces: feelings (pleasant, painful, and neither); perception, memory (of objects: visual, audible, smellable, tasteable, tangible and mental objects); volitional activities (such as those associated and dissociated from consciousness); and consciousness. When we translate "citta" as "mind" this implied Buddhist significance should be remembered.

(56) Sometimes translated as "meditation" which however is too vague a word in English for use in Dharma.

(57) NĪVĀRAṆA—the five hindrances: sensual desire, ill will, sloth and torpor, worry and remorse, scepticism all of which are obstructions to the attainment of the absorptions (dhyāna).

Page 72 (58) The WORLD-ELEMENTS (dhātu) of sensuality, form and formlessness. The first of these comprises, from the "lowest" (spiritually) "upwards:" the hells, animals, hungry ghosts, men and celestials of the sensual realm. In the form world-element are found the celestials of Brahmaloka (the Brahma-gods), as well as those now in their last birth as non-returners (anāgāmi) who attain Nirvāṇa in the Pure Abodes which are the highest planes of this world-element. The formless world-element comprises four states of existence known as infinity of space, etc. Birth in these realms is strictly in accordance with one's karma, i.e. if one allows one's mind to become dominated by lust, birth follows as an animal, if one keeps the Five Precepts one is a man and will be born as one, and if one makes efforts with training, then one will be born upon the level to which one has been successful in training the mind. Only by right application of wisdom can one go beyond the three world elements to experience Nirvāṇa. In Buddhist cosmology, there are innumerable world-elements (lokadhātu) scattered throughout space. In modern terms these would be called galaxies except that the modern and materialist term takes no account of the great range of possibilities for life known to Buddhists.

(59) It is important to note this point and to beware of meditation teachers who stress that "insight" only is enough. Some of them offer "methods" which "guarantee" enlightenment, insight, etc. within a limited time of practice, and some offer a graded series of stages and "interpret" a disciple's progress by his little experiences as representing this or that insight-knowledge (vipaśyana-jñāna).

Page 73 (60) Insight (vipaśyanā) is developed with the five heaps (skandha) as one's basis and with some aspect of them as one's object. The states of absorption and their approaches tend to produce in a meditator all sorts of visions, ecstatic experiences and unsurpassed powers, etc. These things easily lure him off the practice-path which for a Buddhist leads inwards to the nature of the five heaps and not outwards to these distractions. A meditator has to give up all these experiences and use his concentrated mind to penetrate to the marks of the five heaps: Impermanence, duhkha, no-ātman, voidness.

(61) In Theravāda Tradition, the five hindrances oppose entry upon the absorbed states but are in turn opposed one for one by the Five Powers, thus: trust (śraddhā) opposes sensual desire (kāmacchanda); energy (vīrya) opp. ill-will (vyāpāda); mindfulness (sati) opp. sloth and torpor (thīna-middha —styānamiddha, Skt.) collectedness (samādhi) opp. worry and remorse (uddhacca-kukucca); wisdom (paññā) opp. scepticism (vicikicchā).

Page 77 (62) For this process clearly depicted see the large illustrated sheet prepared by the Council for Cultural and Religious Affairs of H. H. the Dalai Lama, reproduced here in miniature.

Page 82 (63) Called " lahutā " (laghutā, Skt.) lightness and grouped in Theravāda Abhidhamma with tranquility, softness (pliancy), adaptability, proficiency and uprightness of both bodily and mental factors.

Page 85 (64) Noble Paths: which are the entry upon the noble (ārya) attainments of Stream-enterer, Once-returner, Non-returner and Arhat, the worthy One.

(65) See notes page 71 (57) and page 73 (61).

Page 86 (66) The passage in the Pāli Suttas upon the first dhyāna many times repeated runs thus: "Detached from sensual objects, O bhikkhus, detached from unskillful states of mind, the bhikkhu enters into the first absorption which is accompanied by thought-conception (vitakka) and thought-examination (vicāra), is born of detachment and filled with joy and bliss (pīti sukha)."

Page 87 (67) The Second Absorption: "After the quietening of thought conception and examination, and by gaining inner tranquility and one-pointedness of mind, he enters into a state free from conception and examination, the second absorption which is born of collectedness (samādhi) and filled with joy and bliss."

(68) The Third Absorption: "After the fading away of joy he dwells in equanimity, mindful, clearly conscious; experiences in his person that feeling of which the Āryas say: 'Happy lives the man of equanimity and attentive mind,' and thus he enters the third absorption."

Page 88 (69) The Fourth Absorption: "After having given up pleasure and pain and through the disappearance of old joys and griefs, he enters into a state beyond pleasure and pain, the fourth absorption, which is purified by equanimity (upekkhā) and mindfulness (sati)."

(70) The Gods or celestial beings exist upon many planes (which are not "up there" in the sky but are

variations of experience due to differences of karma and therefore differences of the sense-organs and hence of varying perception) and these are distinguished as follows:

Sensual-world:

catur-mahārājika-deva: celestials of the Four Great Kings.
trāya-trimśā-deva: celestials of the Thirty-three.
yāmā-deva
tuṣitā-deva
nirmāṇarati-deva
paranirmata-vaśavarti-deva

Form-world:

brahma-pariṣadya
brahma-purohita
mahābrahma

Beings reborn above with weak, medium, or strong 1st dhyāna

parīttābha
apramāṇabha
ābhāsvara

Beings reborn above with weak, medium, or strong 2nd dhyāna

parītta-śubha
apramāṇa-śubha
śubhākṛtsna

Beings reborn above with weak, medium, or strong 3rd dhyāna.

vehapphalā, beings with 4th dhyana reborn here.

asañjnisattva: beings devoid of perception
śuddhāvāsa: the Pure Abodes

Those who have developed the formless attainments and concentrated the mind for the end of perception are reborn in the second, while the third class is only for non-returners who will become Arhats and attain the final quenching in that state.

Page 96 (71) People who adhere to an ātman-view may conceive the physical form as themselves. This is the innate ātman-view grasping at form-heap. Others may " feel " that they have a soul, this being innate ātman-view grasping at the feeling-heap. Memory re-inforces the notion of self and thus there is grasping as perception-memory heap. Others picture the soul as the " seer " behind the sense-organs which resolves itself into grasping at the consciousness heap. The conceptualized views of the theologians and philosophers (grasping at volitions-heap) is of course more subtle and always supported by sophistic arguments.

Page 97 (72) If the ātman's existence is apart from or different from the five heaps, then these cannot be an exhaustive analysis of the personality as claimed by Lord Buddha and the teachers in his tradition: but this would not be supported either by empirical observation, or by the searching penetration resulting from the perfection of wisdom by insight (vipaśyanā). Again, being independent, it could have no relationships—and hence would in any case be unknowable in any way at all. And if its existence is not different or apart from the five heaps, it cannot be independent and hence a contradiction is involved.

Page 98 (73) There is this impressive word of Lord Buddha (*Samyutta-nikāya*, XXII. 47): " All those samanas and brahmins who conceive of a self (ātman) in many ways, conceive it as the five heaps, or as one of them." In conjunction with this section one might well read " The Discourse on the Snake Simile " (*Majjhima-nikāya*, 22) in Nos. 48-49 of the Wheel Publications, from the Buddhist Publication Society, Kandy, Ceylon.

Page 101 (74) See note 28 on page 43. All these conditioning factors arise dependently (not simply by way of cause and effect) and are based upon the brief formulation of Dependent Origination thus: " This being, that is, from the arising of this, that arises. This not being, that is not, from the ceasing of this, that ceases." (imasmiṃ sati, idaṃ hoti; imassuppādā, idam uppajjhati; imasmim asati, idaṃ na hoti; imassa nirodhā, idaṃ nirujjhati.) They are thus void of self nature, relying upon other factors for their origination and decline, and so utterly void.

Page 105 (75) " High " and " low " are used in the sense of relative freedom or bondage, happiness or suffering. Spiritual heights are associated with development, happiness and great (though not ultimate) freedom. The degraded depths (of life in hell and as an animal or hungry ghost, etc.) are conjoined to shrinkage of the mind, and its abilities, to unhappiness and to severe limitations.

Page 106 (76) Of DUHKHA Lord Buddha says that "it should be understood" stressing this in very many discourses, having done this due to the human tendency rooted in the stains, not to want to see or to turn away from seeing duhkha. It may be understood with reference to others but it must be understood within one's "own" mind and body if one wishes for the freedom of Nirvāṇa.

(77) MERITS (puṇya) meaning "that which cleanses and purifies." For instance giving and generosity purify the mind of stinginess, moral conduct purifies the mind of overt evil actions, mind development brings about growth in the mind and the reduction of evil desires. Reverence purifies one of haughtiness, promoting humility, while helpfulness purifies one of callous indifference, promoting compassion. Rejoicing in other's happiness purifies one of envy while promoting muditā (sympathetic joy). Dedicating one's merits for the benefit of others purifies one of the craving for one's salvation alone (without bothering over others) while promoting interest in other's welfare. Listening to the Dharma purifies one of distraction while promoting

concentration. Teaching the Dharma purifies one of selfishness regarding knowledge while promoting friendliness. Setting upright one's views purifies one of views which lead astray (from Dharma) while promoting views tending toward Nirvāṇa. These are the ten ways of making merit frequently taught in Theravāda lands and all of them are essential for balanced Buddhist practice.

Page 107 (78) H. After the Path of Endeavor one enters the Path of Insight and at the moment of doing so, all those stains which are to be destroyed by the latter path, are all burnt up instantly since this Path of Insight is compared to fire. In the attainment of the Path of Insight, the present Path of Endeavor plays an important part. The first stage of the Path of Endeavor is called " uṣmagatā " (heat) because in this stage through development-wisdom having no-ātman as its object, there is a heating of the stains which are later to be destroyed. When this heating becomes intense in the stage of uṣmagatā, this is called " mūrdhana " (summits)—the second stage. After this one reaches the stage of kṣānti (patience), so called because it is able to make extremely hot the stains which are to be destroyed in the Path of Insight. This being accomplished, one is sure to arrive at the Path of Insight and having done so, the gates are closed to birth in realms of woe (apāya-bhūmi). One attains the supreme worldly dharmas (agradharma) and then as a Stream-enterer (śrota-āpanna) starts one's progress through the transcendental levels (lokottara-bhūmi).

Page 108 (79) FIVE SKILLFUL FACULTIES (kuśalendriya) are: Trust, energy, mindfulness, collectedness, and wisdom. Upon becoming guiding powers in the character of an individual, these faculties are called the Five Powers. Trust and wisdom (śraddhā-prajñā), and effort-collectedness (vīrya-samādhi) make up two pairs and perfect balance is needed in the development of these if one would become an accomplished Buddhist, "Mindfulness (smṛti), I declare, O bhikkhus, is helpful everywhere." (*Samyutta-nikāya*, 46, 53.)

(80) FOUR NOBLE TRUTHS in 16 aspects:

- i acceptance of the truth of Duhkha in the realm of sensuality
- ii conviction about this Truth
- iii that this is true also for the Realm of Form
- iv as well as for the Formless Realm
- v acceptance of the truth of the Arising of Duhkha
- vi conviction about this Truth
- vii that this is true also for the Realm of Form
- viii as well as for the Formless Realm
- ix acceptance of the Truth of the Cessation of Duhkah
- x conviction about this Truth
- xi that this is true also for the Realm of Form
- xii as well as for the Formless Realm
- xiii acceptance of the Truth of the Practice-path leading to Cessation of Duhkha

xiv conviction about this Truth
xv that this is true also for the Realm of Form
xvi as well for the Formless Realm.

It is obvious that these are intended as insight meditations producing renunciation of the whole of the wandering-on (saṃsāra).

Page 109 (81) Here the supermundane path is described but this Eightfold Path may also be (as in Theravāda) very much the basis of ordinary day to day Buddhist life. The explanation of the eight factors given here differs almost entirely from those found in the Pāli *Sutta Piṭaka.* For these Sutta explanations, see *Word of the Buddha* by Ven. Nyānatiloka Mahāthera, Buddhist Publication Society, Kandy, Ceylon.

(82) As described this factor will be the equivalent of the ariyavācā (noble speech) in Pāli, which is also concerned with the Dharma and leads those who hear it and engage in it, to great profit, even to becoming a noble one (ārya): see *Dīgha-nikaya,* Sutta 33, v, xxv. (The Recital, Dialogues of the Buddha, vol. III.)

Page 110 (83) The divisions of the Path found in the Pāli Discourses are simple: first two factors—wisdom (prajñā), the next three—virtue (śīla), and the last three —collectedness (samādhi). It thus embraces the whole range of the Threefold training.

Page 112 (84) these Six Perfections are:

1	dāna	giving	upaya-kauśalya (skillful means)	puṇya-saṃbhāra (burden of merits)
2	śīla	virtue		
3	kṣānti	patience		
4	vīrya	endeavor		
5	samādhi	collectedness		
6	prajñā	wisdom	prajñā	jñāna-saṃbhāra (the burden of wisdom)

Ten perfections are found in later Pāli literature:

1	dāna	giving
2	sīla	virtue
3	nekkhamma	renunciation
4	paññā	wisdom
5	adhitthāna	determination
6	viriya	energy
7	khanti	patience
8	sacca	truthfulness
9	mettā	friendliness
10	upekkhā	equanimity

In both cases these virtues are for the cultivation of one who aspires to be a Buddha practicing the Bodhisattva path. The latter is also taught and practiced in Theravāda countries, the Jātaka stories providing good material for illustrating the bodhisattva's path.

Page 113 (85) "All Beings" can have various meanings. To start with even a Buddha is only able to lead all *tamable* beings to freedom. A good example of an untamable being is found in the naked ascetic Upaka whom Lord Buddha met after enlightenment and on his way to Benares, the deer park at Isipaṭṭaṇa. Beings with few roots of merit and much delusion (moha) will be unlikely to be able to understand Dharma. " All beings " also received a very practical interpretation in the hands of some meditation teachers. They have specially emphasized that " all beings " means the variety of different " people " which are displayed in one's own character. Thus, the kind person, the angry person, the generous person, the stingy person, and so forth, all these aspects of one's own character should be led to Nirvāṇa. Or it may be explained in terms of the six spheres of birth, all of which are potential and sometimes actual in one's own mind (celestials, men, titans, hungry ghosts, animals and hell-wraiths). Or again, the perception of " beings " to be led to Nirvāṇa takes place where?—in one's own mind.

(86) The progress of the bodhisattva gathering merits is well illustrated in the *Jātaka*, or Birth stories which are related as the previous lives of Gotama the Buddha. People often object that it is doubtful whether these are in fact his previous births but in doubting thus they lose the point of the stories all of which contain lessons for noble and altruistic conduct. As one often learns better from the examples of characters in stories, than from treatises, so these Jātakas and other Buddhist stories should be read in the spirit of " What can I learn for the living of my life from these stories?"

(87) In the meditative states in which it is able to do this, one has to bear in mind two apparently opposing ideas: first, that it is skillful to pay respect and listen

to Dharma in any case and very skillful when one is concerned with Buddhas; and second, that all the Buddhas and bodhisattvas are after all perceived in one's mind. Nevertheless, one respects them as a way of developing humility and ability to hear the Dharma.

Page 114 (88) See note page 12 (1).

(89) There are interesting accounts of bhikṣus in all Buddhist countries who have tamed rough and uncontrollable men. Even more striking are the stories of bhikṣus who have tamed animals giving them the Refuges and the Precepts so that thereafter they lived peaceful lives not harming others.

Page 115 (90) There is an interesting comparison here with the Arahant who is also able to change his feelings as he pleases. This power, called Āriya-iddhi [Ārya-siddhi, Skt.] (noble magic) is only possessed by the noble ones, among them, the Arahants. One who enters the attainment of cessation (nirodha-samāpatti) also cannot be affected by fire nor come to any danger from weapons. It is also a characteristic of one who practices and is successful with friendliness (mettā—maitrī, Skt.), that he is preserved from fire, poisons and weapons. Naturally, both the bodhisattva and the Arahant have practiced and are accomplished in friendliness toward all beings.

Page 116 (91) CATU-SANGAHA-VATTHU (catur-samgraha-vastu, Skt.) a group of dharmas occurring many times in the Pāli Canon as the way of practice for, and the mark of, the noble disciple (Āriyasavaka). These four are very often the subject of discourses given to the lay people in Siam where they are much appreciated as qualities of the true Buddhist.

Page 117 (92) See note page 112 (84).

Page 118 (93) An interesting parallel is found here in all schools of Buddhist practice: " Practice in this life, attain in this life " could well be the motto of all Buddhist meditation teachers whether they follow the traditions of Theravāda, Vajrayāna, or Ch'an (Zen).

(94) This is the selection of and practice with the aid of the form of a celestial being—Buddha, bodhisattva or some protector-god. Details and methods vary and must be obtained from a teacher but in essence all the practices resemble what is taught in Theravāda in that they help one to realize that the five heaps are void and that the dharmas too into which they may be divided are also void. Much resemblance might be seen between these devayoga practices and the ancient practices employing colored discs (kasina), for which see the *Path of Purification*, (English translation of the *Visuddhimagga*), Semage and Co., Colombo, Ceylon.

(95) KRIYA-TANTRA: which instructs in ritual and exterior modes of worship for the accumulation of merits, and are suited to those of dull faculties. Ubhayacaryā-tantra, have both ritual instructions and some interior

mind-development practices. Yoga-tantra embody more instructions for meditation practice and contain little on ritual, while Anuttarayoga-tantra are for those of the sharpest faculties and concentrate only upon interior collectedness and perception of the void.

(96) The same privacy is often found in Theravāda when a teacher gives meditation instructions to a disciple. This is not because there is anything to be hidden (for which reason the use of the word "secret" should be avoided), but because, upon occasion, individual pupils require individual attention. The division of Buddhists into "esoteric" and "exoteric" is a nonsensical relic of a misunderstanding fifty years or more old. What is hidden from us, is hidden by ignorance and stupidity in our own minds.

Page 119 (97) This one unambiguous sentence should help to destroy the very mistaken views which many people hold regarding Tāntric practice in the Vajrayāna. Even learned professors have been known to remark that it is possible by way of Tāntric practice to gain Buddhahood without relinquishing anything at all, what to speak of the confused views of the less learned. The way of one who wishes to practice earnestly is, as with all paths in the Dharma, a hard one. In Tibet formerly, Tāntrikas frequently withdrew into solitary abodes, such as mountain caves, for years at a time. This very practice refutes the wrong views.

(98) This in itself means that advanced meditation practices are for those " advanced " in a Buddhist sense; that is, those possessing strong roots of skill and a stable personality. Those not so advanced must start on the lower but very essential levels of making merit, such as giving and keeping pure the precepts.

(99) One should always have a teacher if one wishes to practice meditation. It is desirable even if one wishes to study a Buddhist treatise to have a teacher to guide one in the tradition but it is nearly always necessary with meditation practice. The prime mark of a good teacher is that he has already accomplished whatever he teaches. Robes and rituals fascinate people but these are not necessarily marks of a teacher. What is necessary for certain progress along the path leading to enlightenment, is that one receives guidance at the hand of a teacher who has already gone along that path, if not to the end, at least to within sight of the end.

(100) This is another most important point. There are those who imagine that it is only in Theravāda that the precepts are kept, thinking that Mahāyāna is slack in this respect, but strictness and slackness depends not on " yāna " but upon the teacher. Others again imagine that the Tantras offer a spiritual path where moral conduct is not required and where consequently one may do anything. Neither of these ideas

is anything like the truth. It is true to say anywhere in Buddhist tradition "the more intensive the training, the stricter the precepts." Dhūtaṅga bhikṣus in a Siamese jungle-wat, Zen monks in their temples or Tāntrikas high in their hermitages, must all, because of their striving, keep pure the precepts.

(101) Such as upon one of the many Tibetan painted scrolls, or in the form of images, all of which may be used as an exterior support. Later, the same design is visualized complete internally. See note page 12 (3).

Page 120 (102) It is possible to discern in the Pāli Discourses, the seeds out of which this teaching has grown. For the Dharmakāya, there are rare statements such as "He who sees Dhamma, sees me" (*Samyutta-nikāya*, III. 120). Then the Sambhogakāya seems to be connected with the body of the Buddha exhibiting the 32 marks of a great person. Obviously, like the Sambhogakāya, it was not visible to all but only seen by some persons. The Rūpakāya of Nirmāṇakāya would find its equivalent in the ordinary body seen by every one, the physical form of Gotama which sat in meditation, walked to collect food and so forth, but which in the words of Lord Buddha could not be identified (*Samyutta-nikāya*, III. 111 and IV. 383) as the Buddha. Some teachers of meditation have stressed this teaching as having a practical importance, the three (or four) Buddha bodies all lying within one's own mind.

Page 122 (103) The 37 BODHIPAKṢIKADHARMA (varga) comprises the following groups:

4 Applications of Mindfulness	(smṛtyupasthāna)
4 Right Efforts	(samyakprahāna)
4 Paths to Psychic power	(ṛddhipāda)
5 Faculties	(indriya)
5 Powers	(bala)
7 Factors of Enlightenment	(bodhyaṅga)
8-fold Way	(mārga)

For a Theravāda explanation see the *Buddhist Dictionary* published in Ceylon by Frewin & Co., Colombo.

Page 123 (104) The southern continent of the ancient Indian world system.

(105) These are frequently the subject of very beautiful sets of painted scrolls.

Page 125 (106) A similar but uncanonical story is the reason for the gorgeously adorned Buddhas to be found both in Burma and in Siam. In this case a haughty prince was subdued by Lord Buddha after the latter had shown himself transformed into a " universal-righteous-emperor " (cakravarti-rāja).

(107) In Theravāda commentaries, he is called Santussita Devarāja.

Page 127 (108) See *Majjhima-nikāya*, I. 395, where it is said that the Tathāgata:

does not speak the false, useless, unpleasant,
does not speak the true, useless, unpleasant,
does speak *at the right time*: the true, useful, unpleasant,

does not speak the false, useless, pleasant,
does not speak the true, useless, pleasant,
does speak *at the right time*: true, useful, pleasant.

Page 128 (109) In Pāli Suttas see *Aṅguttara-nikāya*, V. 32ff.; *Majjhima-nikāya*, I. 69; and *Milindapañha*, 105, 285. These are very similar but not quite the same as the list in this work.

Page 129 (110) In Pāli Suttas see *Majjhima-nikāya*, I. 71ff. These four are exactly the same in Pāli.

Page 131 (111) In Pāli Suttas see *Majjhima-nikāya*, III. 221, for a similar list.

(112) For these, see *Aṅguttara-nikāya*, IV. 82, where "livelihood" is mentioned as a fourth factor in the group.

Page 135 (113) On the question of the All-knowing-knowledge, (Pāli: sabbaññutāñāṇa). It is clear from a study of the most ancient Pāli texts that in them Lord Buddha never claimed omniscience. Later Pāli treatises such as the *Patisambhidāmagga* contain elaborate accounts of how the Buddha is omniscient. In *Majjhima-nikāya*, I. 482, Lord Buddha specifically disclaims that he is omniscient and all-seeing while stressing that he has the threefold knowledge (tisso vijjā).

Page 137 (114) The same spirit is found in the *Majjhima-nikāya* where Lord Buddha disclaims that he must reflect before teaching.

Page 139 (115) See note page 26 (17).

In these notes, references to Pāli texts, are to those issued by the Pali Text Society, London. As most of these texts have now been translated into English, they may be read in English as well. Also important as a source of genuine information on "root-Dharma" mostly from Pāli sources, is the Buddhist Publication Society, Kandy, Ceylon. For further reading upon the Life of His Holiness the Dalai Lama, see *My Land and My People* (Asia Publishing House, Bombay and New Delhi). For guidance as to reliable works on Tibetan form of the Dharma, as well as upon Tibetan affairs generally, apply to the: Bureau of His Holiness the Dalai Lama, 15 Link Road, New Delhi 14; or to: Council of Cultural and Religious Affairs of His Holiness the Dalai Lama, Gangchen Kyishong, Sessions Road, Dharamsala, District Kangra, Himachal Pradesh, India.